EVERY MAN'S
GUIDE ᴛᴏ
OUTDOOR

SURVIVAL

EVERY MAN'S GUIDE TO OUTDOOR SURVIVAL

DALE MARTIN

Horizon Publishers
Springville, Utah

ISBN 13: 978-0-88290-977-6

Published by Horizon Publishers, an imprint of Cedar Fort, Inc., 2373 W. 700 S., Springville, UT 84663
Distributed by Cedar Fort, Inc. www.cedarfort.com

LIBRARY OF CONGRESS CATALOGING-IN-PUBLICATION DATA

Martin, Dale.
  Every man's guide to outdoor survival : book 1 : from primitive food
gathering to armchair-stocked comfort / Dale Martin.
     p. cm.
  ISBN 978-0-88290-977-6
  1. Wilderness survival. I. Title.

  GV200.5.M367 2010
  613.6'9--dc22

2010041694

Cover design by Megan Whittier
Cover design © 2011 by Lyle Mortimer
Edited and typeset by Megan E. Welton

Printed in the United States of America

10 9 8 7 6 5 4 3 2 1

Printed on acid-free paper

To my wife, Sue.

"When people call you lucky, it's usually because you prepared for something that they didn't."

—Unknown

"Learning is not compulsory. . . . neither is survival."
—W. Edwards Deming

"Sometimes a tactical retreat is not a bad response. . . . first, you survive."

—Lois McMaster Bujold

CONTENTS

SECTION THREE: THE REALLY WORST-CASE SCENARIO

INTRODUCTION

Getting at what this book is all about may take a few paragraphs of explanation, starting with a few paragraphs of what
this book is not.

It is not one of those "grab a gun and head for the hills" survival books. There are probably enough of those around already.
At any rate, that type of living is impractical because most of us
have jobs, children, school, or responsibilities of some sort.

Nor is this one of those "how to live on roots and berries for
the next year" books. Again, for most of us, that is impractical.

Nor is it a "prediction" book, telling you exactly what the
future holds and all the things you need to do to avoid the impend-
ing disaster. I don't know *for sure* what's going to happen. Neither
does anyone else.

But, having said that, there *is* a section of this book that deals
with retreating to wilderness areas for safety in the event of a complete societal collapse.

There *is* a section on primitive food gathering, fire building,
and water filtering.

There *is* a section on trying to assess the most likely potential
threats to our welfare.

This book is much like a fire extinguisher. As long as nothing negative happens to our economy or society in general, the

information contained in this book wouldn't be absolutely vital. It would be good to know but maybe not vital. Also like keeping a fire extinguisher on hand—just in case—if something does happen, the items and skills described in this book could be extremely critical.

Not knowing exactly what the future holds, this book gives a broad overview of survival information that is *situation oriented*— information that could be essential to surviving in some instances might be literally worthless in others and vice versa.

Uses for this book might include

1. General, around-the-house living to supplement the family table where no actual "survival" situation exists
2. Do's and don'ts related to stockpiling for possible future hard times
3. Taking weekend or short-term excursions into the country for the purpose of reaping wild resources to supplement your family's welfare
4. Survival when unexpectedly stranded in remote areas with few resources and you find yourself in an actual life-or-death situation
5. Heaven forbid, survival when retreating for your own personal safety to remote areas (even short term) to weather a full-scale socioeconomic collapse in which there are few resources to buy or no money with which to buy them.

The potential threats out there are also almost endless. From terrorist attacks to asteroid impacts, many things are *possible*, although some are a lot more likely than others.

The most likely threat to most of us Joe Average North Americans is a drastic economic slowdown, or worse, a complete economic collapse as in 1929. Most of us are no longer mentally equipped to deal with really hard and lean times. We have all lived the good life for so long that if something like the Great Depression happens in today's world, it will be one heck of a wake-up call.

The economy of the United States, and indeed the world, is being talked about as never before. For the last sixty-plus years since World War II, economists and government officials have confidently told us that the crash of 1929 and the following Great Depression can't happen again. There are too many safeguards in our banking and financial systems.

I sincerely hope they prove to be correct. I further hope that the financial meltdown we have been watching since 2008 turns around and things smooth out. Like the Joe Average North American that this book is written for, I greatly prefer living comfortably in my home, shopping at the grocery store, and enjoying electricity, air conditioning, TV, hot water, and so forth.

But people are already nervous. For the last several months, many different types of normally common ammunition has become almost totally unavailable, even at places like Walmart. And this a nationwide occurrence. It isn't that hunting ammunition is no longer being manufactured; it is simply being bought up as soon as it is put on the shelves.

In addition, the housing, auto manufacturing, and banking systems are in dire straits. Unemployment has been steadily rising for months with no end in sight.

Our "wonderful" government decided to rectify all of these problems by going on a spending spree and bailing out everyone in sight. (And we thought we were in debt before.) We can only hope that all these societal debacles will turn around and go in a more positive direction.

Nonetheless, I like to be prepared for any eventual "what-ifs" that might occur. This book is about surviving, improvising, retreating if necessary, planning for the future, and reaping outdoor resources. It contains the basics of weathering tumultuous times using mostly common sense and a few old-time and almost forgotten skills, along with ideas about food and medicinal stockpiling with particular attention to expiration issues, and a fair dose of what we can all do without greatly affecting our lifestyle.

The first half of the book will deal with more primitive survival-type information on how to reap wild resources. This part of the book assumes you are forced by circumstance into having to use primitive equipment to reap these wild resources, or that you are using these primitive methods to save money for other considerations. Obviously, better equipment and planning ahead would make this resource gathering task much easier. This information would still be useful; the job would just be easier with more efficient equipment.

The second half of the book deals with preparing well enough in advance so that no matter what scenario develops, you will be ahead of the game. This section will have a large measure of information about stockpiling and survival packs and general forward thinking.

I hope this book makes interesting reading and that the information contained makes us all feel at least a little more comfortable about future "what if" situations. This book follows the old adage, "Hope and pray for the best, but prepare for the worst." If the worst happens, you'll feel a little more confident than most. If it doesn't, you'll be happy about that too.

Best regards,
Dale Martin

SECTION ONE
BASIC
SURVIVAL

CHAPTER ONE
TO BUILD A FIRE

There is something about a campfire that is primal and hard-wired into the human genome. How many times on a camping trip have you heard someone say something on the order of: "I like sitting by the campfire and looking into the flames"?

Even if the group is sitting twenty feet away from a forty-foot Winnebago, and the campfire is not necessary at all, many people still build one. The campfire means comfort and reassurance, regardless of whether it is really essential for any other purpose.

On a more serious note, building a fire does have a lot of practical and generally obvious uses:

- Warmth for cold weather and hot coals for a cooking fire would be the most common reasons to build a fire.
- Campfire light at night enhances the experience as opposed to a dark camp.
- A fire is essential for boiling water to drink in survival situations.
- A fire can also keep potentially dangerous wild animals at bay if that is a problem.
- Signaling a rescuer to your location can be accomplished by tossing greenery on your fire to create thickly visible smoke.

I hope we will always have survival items for fire starting in our backpacks, but the following are a few of the more primitive methods of getting a fire going if the situation dictates.

WHAT ABOUT TINDER?

Tinder is something that is easily inflammable to help get a fire going long enough for the larger pieces of wood to catch fire. Like almost everything in this book, tinder is situation oriented.

If you have only one or two matches and are out in a cold environment where a fire is essential to your staying alive or freezing to death, then tinder is *deathly important*.

If, on the other hand, you are in the same situation, but you have a Bic lighter in your pocket that will light a thousand times before running out of fuel, then tinder considerably lessens in significance.

However, even in the second situation, to get a fire going reasonably quickly, the use of tinder is key.

Counter-clockwise from top: dryer lint, dry pine straw, pine cones, birds' nest, fuzz stick, and small sticks.

A variety of materials—both from the "wild" as well as items found around the house that you can take with you in advance—can be used as tinder. Of course, there are a lot of commercially available fire starting aids at any outdoor store, but the tinder shown in this book is either from the wild or adapted from common household items.

Fuzz Sticks: Fuzz sticks are simply dry sticks about six inches long and no more than one inch in diameter that are carved out along their length with a knife to produce shavings that are still attached to the shaft of the stick. They are usually used four or five at a time. When stacked together, the match (or whatever flame source) has lots of thin slivers of wood to ignite and burn instead of just the smooth one-inch diameter stick that would be hard to ignite without it being "fuzzed."

Ideally, the cuts in the wood should be as long as possible, but yet still leave the slivers of wood attached to the stick. The longer the slivers, the more air can get between them and the main shaft of the stick to aid ignition.

Fuzz stick

Birds' Nests: A ready-made tinder source that you can find almost anywhere. Start by looking in bushes and shrubs, not tall trees. Even thick and heavy birds' nests are made of relatively small sticks and are generally reasonably dry, even after a rain. The inside of most nests is usually covered with a soft and fine layer of dry grass, which is also a good igniter. With your hands, crumble some more dry grass to an almost powderlike consistency and put the powdery flakes of dry grass into the nest, partially filling it. Collect several of these if you can.

PINE CONES AND PINE STRAW: A pine cone is a naturally occurring fuzz stick. If you are in an area of pine trees, you can usually pick these up off the ground. Most of the time they are dry enough to use, even if the ground is damp. Like the man-made fuzz stick, there is lots of air space and thin slivers of the cone to easily ignite.

Pine straw is equally good tinder. Again, unlike picking up fire wood that has been laying on the ground and is generally too water logged to use, pine straw will almost always be dry enough to burn. Simply ball it up with your hands to allow air to pass through it, and it will ignite.

DRY GRASS: Rather than just using dry grass in stalks, bend them into a circle about the size of a softball and fill in the center with more dry grass. You are, in essence, making a bird nest. Crumble up more dry grass into a fine powder to fill in the bottom of the "nest." The reason that the bottom of the nest needs to be fairly dense is that most primitive fire starting methods generate a small ember or coal that must be fanned into a fire. You need to be able to drop the tiny ember into the ball of dry grass without the ember falling completely through and being wasted.

SMALL STICKS: Usually the best sticks to use as tinder are small dead limbs picked off trees and shrubs that are still standing. Quite often, those picked up directly from the ground are waterlogged. Get more than you think you'll need (at least fifty or so) that are 6- to 12-inches long but no bigger around than ¼-inch or so. If all you can find are larger in diameter, split them if possible. As with all the items above, the aim is to give the fire more surface area to catch rather than trying to light a single large limb.

HEART PINE: If you are in an area where there are pine trees, there will likely be at least a few pine stumps around that will be what the old timers called "heart pine" or "rich pine." Rich pine is probably a better name for it since this material doesn't necessarily come from the center, or heart, of the tree.

There is probably a more technical or scientific name for it, but it is essentially the part of the pine that still contains the inflammable resin and does not rot away like most of the tree will do.

Quite often you will see a stump of a long-since dead pine tree sticking out of the ground a few inches or maybe even a foot or so tall. (I usually find them by tripping over them.)

Stump containing rich pine—most likely no more than 2 years old.

What is left of the stump (even after twenty or thirty years) is typically hard as a rock, but you can chip away small slivers with a hunting knife or even a rock, if necessary. These small slivers of wood will ignite almost like gasoline. I have never seen a better naturally occurring tinder. The appearance of this heart pine is usually one of two colors.

If the stump is only a few years old (thirty or less), the inside will still be yellow in color. I am not a forestry expert by any means, but a forest ranger once told me that this sap or resin is turpentine. Turpentine is a substance naturally produced by pine trees, so this may be the answer.

If the stump is much older than thirty years, it will look gray, even on the inside. It is still very good tinder, even at this stage, and will ignite quickly, although not quite as well as if it still had the yellowish color.

Same stump chipped away to reveal yellowish rich pine. The color and smell are unmistakable.

DRYER LINT: Although it burns up fairly quickly once sparked, dryer lint makes pretty good initial tinder to get your teepee of small sticks going, and you generate enough of it drying clothes anyway. In fact, I bet up until now, you just threw it away.

OILY OR GAS-SOAKED RAGS: This method should be reserved for very limited circumstances, such as being stranded near a disabled car or downed aircraft in a remote and cold environment.

In such a rare instance, one can usually wipe enough oil from engine parts to get a rag relatively saturated with oil or by getting oil off the dipstick.

To get gas, use a long vacuum hose from the engine to siphon some gas out of the tank. Even if you've run out of gas, there will still be enough in the tank to wet a rag. You might also try undoing the fuel line under the hood to get gas on the rag. If you have a wire coat hanger, attach the rag to one end and run it into the gas tank. You don't need much gas on the rag for it to be a good tinder.

RUBBING ALCOHOL RAG: If you are stranded by a disabled car or downed aircraft, you can often find a first aid kit. Many people carry a kit in their car, and kits are in virtually all aircraft. If there is a small bottle of alcohol, soak a rag or even a paper towel with the alcohol. Roll it into a fairly tight ball and light it. The fumes emanating from the rag ball will burn fairly well, even in a wind.

Keep in mind, however—the devil is in the details, you know—that you shouldn't soak the rag or paper towel with the alcohol until you are ready to light it because the alcohol will evaporate into the air fairly quickly.

PAPER: Ball up each sheet into golf ball-sized (or bigger) wads to aid ignition. Again, some sort of paper can usually be found in most cars or aircraft.

FIRE-STARTING METHODS

All of the following methods will assume you have already made or acquired some form of tinder as described above.

MAGNIFYING GLASS: This method is fairly obvious, but there are details and variations. Almost any type of magnifying glass will start a fire without much trouble by simply focusing the sun's light on the tinder. It takes a fairly steady hand and sometimes a full minute or more—depending on conditions—for the tinder to start to smoke.

Starting a fire with a magnifying glass will take a little longer in cold weather. It is easiest (by far) if the sun is directly overhead. The dryness of the tinder also comes into play, obviously. The steadier you can focus the lens, the faster your fire will start.

Regardless of these variables, Joe Average North American out there will normally have little trouble getting a fire going with this method.

Magnifying glass

Variation: If the situation is desperate, there are lenses in binoculars and cameras. Of course, use of these lenses may entail destroying your binoculars or camera to get the lenses out, but the scenario may arise that would warrant such an action. An irregularly shaped piece of broken glass can *sometimes* be used for this purpose.

Use the lens of binoculars to light kindling.

I cringe every time I read in a survival manual that people are told they have to tear up their binoculars to get the lens out. It is a bit more difficult to use binoculars as a magnifying glass to start a fire because it is harder to focus the light on the tinder. Regardless, Joe Average North American will find the method easy enough to accomplish.

Point the big end of the binoculars toward the sun. The slight difficulty will be in getting the binoculars pointed exactly at the sun, thereby concentrating the sun's rays to a fine point on the tinder. It sounds easy, but it is a little harder than using a traditional magnifying glass. It's one of those things that you learn by doing. Try it out on the next sunny day.

With cameras, it depends on how the camera is made and whether it would have to be destroyed to use the lens. If you can manage to get access to your camera lens, starting the fire will work in the same way the binoculars do.

Using even a cheap, plastic magnifying glass will effectively start a fire using rich pine, as shown above.

CONDOM: Assuming the condom is clear in color, it can be filled with water and used in exactly the same manner as the magnifying glass above. The difference is, of course, that the water-filled condom is flexible—not rigid like a magnifying glass. Therefore, you will have to shape the condom with your fingers into a "lens" shape, and hold it that way long enough for the light to focus to a fine point to ignite the tinder.

Use a condom to light kindling.

Using a condom is more difficult because not only do you have to hold it at the right focal length, but you also have to hold the condom in the right shape. Nonetheless, it can be done. Substitutes for the condom might include plastic wrap, clear balloons, plastic baggies, and so on.

This method is definitely more difficult for most of us than using a magnifying glass. A variant of this method is to use two rings (like you would find to hang a shower curtain) that are two inches or less in diameter. Hold the condom in between the rings, and allow the rings to hold the condom of water into a more perfect lens shape than you can do with just your fingers.

Even with rich pine, focus must be held for a good two

minutes, which is longer than most of us can hold steady for. This is a difficult method to master.

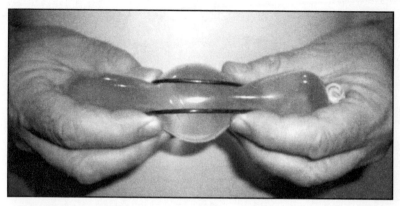

Use shower rings to shape condom into a lens shape.

ICE LENS: This is one of the few things in this book I have not tried personally, and frankly, I would consider it a long shot at best.

Using a rubber band, fasten plastic wrap (or similar material) around the top of a can. Then pour water onto the plastic wrap. If the plastic wrap is fastened loosely enough, the water will freeze into half an ice lens. You will need two of these pieces to form the complete lens.

The trick is to keep close watch and use the lens before bubbles form in the center, which will happen if the water freezes too hard. Bubbles will mess up the light refraction. Ignite tinder in the same manner as a magnifying glass or other lens.

Another method is to find a piece of ice from a stream or creek and carve it as close to a lens shape as you can. Once you start approaching your desired shape, use the warmth of your hands to finish shaping and smoothing the lens.

One obvious downside to the ice lens method is the loss of body heat while you are trying to shape the lens.

MAGNESIUM/FLINT: This is a store-bought item, but it's very small and will easily fit unnoticeably in your pocket.

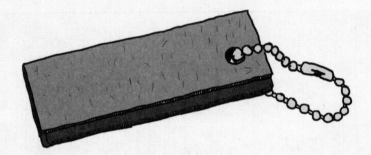

Magnesium/flint bar: Striking the flint at the bottom with nearly anything metal—the back of your knife, even a clothes zipper—will generate sparks to light the magnesium.

Many people find flint much less troublesome to carry than matches for several reasons. It is less bothersome than carrying fifteen or twenty matches, *and* this magnesium and flint combination will light dozens (probably hundreds) of fires. It doesn't matter if the flint gets wet, and the bar is practically unbreakable.

Use a knife to shave magnesium into a pile. The larger the pile of shavings, the easier it will be to start your fire. Remember, magnesium burns fast and intense, so make sure you have your good tinder ready.

A bar of magnesium with a flint attached to one side works by shaving off little slivers of the magnesium and then using the back side of your knife against the flint to create a spark onto the tiny pile of shavings.

The magnesium shavings will ignite easily and burn intensely, so have your tinder ready.

Almost anything metal—such as the back of a knife or a clothes zipper—will generate sparks when struck against the flint. Sometimes even striking a rock against the flint will work. Overall, this method is very easy for nearly anyone.

FLINT/STEEL: Before magnesium starters came along, the basic same method was used to directly ignite the tinder.

Strike the back of your knife against the flint, creating sparks to ignite your tinder.

This method eliminates the need for the magnesium bar shavings in the previous example, but the tinder has to be good and dry (almost powdery) in order for the sparks to ignite it.

The flint/steel method might be more difficult for most of us Joe Average North Americans than using magnesium.

By the way, an empty butane lighter will still have a small spark-generating flint inside it. Also, actual flint (the stone, not commercially made flint) like the Native Americans used to make arrowheads will generate sparks when banged together, although this type of stone is not always easy to find.

BOW AND SPINDLE: This method, like a lot of things in life, is considerably more difficult than it appears when you are observing someone else do it. Even the old pros sometimes have difficulty with it, especially if conditions are not favorable (wind, marginal tinder, damp terrain, and so forth). Details and technique definitely count in the ease (or difficulty) of getting a fire going using this method.

The bow and spindle method is one you might want to practice in advance. You'll have a lot more confidence if you ever really "had to" build a fire in this manner if you've already successfully used the method at home.

There are five components to the bow and spindle set: (1) the bow, (2) the spindle, (3) the foot board, (4) the hand board, and (5) the string.

There are probably innumerable species of wood you can use for these components, but cedar is hard to beat for several reasons. First, it can usually be found in almost any forest in North America and is most often found in a dead tree or in dead tree limbs. A small (6 foot or so), dead cedar tree will remaining standing for years before actually it falls and begins decaying. Even after a cedar has fallen, parts of the wood will remain dry and hard for a long time. This property works well for a bow and spindle set, especially the spindle.

Other woods that work are spruce, poplar, fir, and aspen. I haven't tried oak, but it stands to reason that it would work.

THE BOW—Find a tree branch with a ¾-inch diameter and that is 18 to 24 inches long. The bow must be curved slightly so that when you attach the string, the string will be about 2 inches from where your hand holds the bow. This 2-inch distance is important.

The bow can be a "live" branch or a dead limb, as long as it is still somewhat flexible. The footboard, hand board, and spindle need to be hard, dry wood.

THE SPINDLE—This item only needs to be about 8 inches long and relatively round, much like a short piece of wood dowel, and only the width of your finger in diameter. Sharpen the spindle to a point on both ends, but only at approximately a 45-degree angle, not sharply pointed like a spear. Then round off one end as much as possible. This rounded end will be the top. The spindle needs to be dry, hard wood.

THE FOOT BOARD—This item should be a relatively flat board about a foot or so long and at least 2 inches wide. In the

REMEMBER:

- SPINDLE MUST BE MADE FROM HARDER WOOD THAN FOOT BOARD.

- BOW SHOULD HAVE A SLIGHT CURVE TO ENSURE AT LEAST A 2-INCH GAP BETWEEN THE STRING AND YOUR HAND.

- BOW CAN BE GREEN, BUT HANDBOARD, FOOT-BOARD, AND SPINDLE MUST BE DRY!

HANDBOARD

4 INCHES

SPINDLE

8 INCHES

FOOTBOARD

12 INCHES

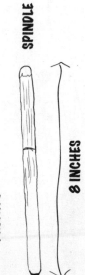

BOW

18 to 24 INCHES

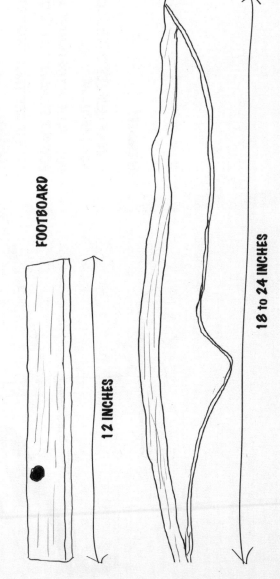

REMEMBER:

- SPINDLE MUST BE ON THE OUTSIDE OF BOWSTRING, NOT THE INSIDE.

- CUT A SLOT IN THE FOOTBOARD TO ALLOW POWDER TO ACCUMULATE TO EMBER BELOW.

- GATHER DRY TINDER UNDER FOOTBOARD TO CATCH EMBERS.

- BE PATIENT! IT TAKES 30 SECONDS OR SO TO CREATE SMOKE, AND ANOTHER FEW MINUTES TO CREATE EMBER.

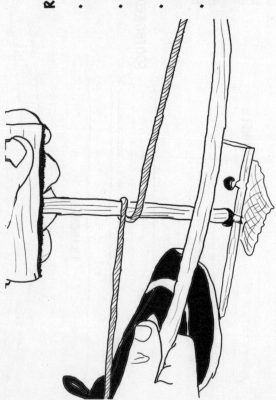

wild, you may have to split some branches to get a board at least somewhat flat (like a piece of lumber). It needs to be about ½ inch thick. *Critical:* The footboard needs to be made of a softer wood than the spindle. If your spindle is cedar, try using pine for the foot board.

The Hand Board—This item needs to be identical to the foot board but shorter in length—only 4 inches. Round it off around the edges for more comfort when holding and drill out an depression for the top of the spindle. This depression should be in the exact center of the hand board.

The String—This item should be a length of thick cotton cordage about ¼ inch in diameter. However, nearly any type of string material will work, but thicker is better. Regular shoe or boot strings may work once or twice, but they will probably snap with repeated uses. Some nylon cords, especially if too thin, will overheat and melt. Narrow leather straps will work.

Carve a depression into the foot board for the bottom of the spindle to fit into, but do so only about a spindle's width from the edge of the board and closer to the end of the foot board because your foot will cover most of the opposite end.

To start, place the bow and spindle set-up over something to catch the embers you will generate.

Make sure the spindle is on the outside of the bow, not the inside. Turn the bow at a slight downward angle, not horizontal with the ground. If the spindle is on the inside of the bow, it is constantly banging on both ends of the bow and decreases the speed you can build up.

If the bow is not held at an angle, the cord will rub against itself along the spindle, again decreasing your maximum speed.

Gradually build up smoothness and speed in your back-and-forth motion until the ends of the spindle smolder and turn dark. A little smoke will gradually appear. If possible, grease the top end of the spindle with oil from your hair, facial oil around the nose, or anything else you might have. The aim is to decrease friction (and heat) at the top of the spindle while generating the heat at the bottom end of the spindle.

When the bottom of the spindle and the footboard are both scorched brown and the first wisps of smoke appear, cut a notch from the edge of the foot board to the edge of the spindle depression. This will give the powder created by the spindle turning a place to accumulate. Eventually, the ember will be generated here.

Once the ember is generated, dump it into your tinder and gently blow on it to light the tinder. It usually takes 30 seconds or so to get the footboard smoking enough to create burning powder. It will take another couple of minutes to create the ember. It is a more exhausting task than it would seem.

SODA CAN AND CANDY BAR: This method isn't as crazy as it sounds, but it is extremely difficult and may be a "last resort" method. Relative to some of the previous methods, this one is tough for Joe Average North American.

The bottom of the soda can is used as a reflector to focus the sun's rays on a *tiny* piece of tinder held on the end of a toothpick-sized stick. This tiny piece of tinder is held at the exact focal point of the reflector.

I used a tiny piece of rich pine to see if it would ignite without any luck. The soda can reflector turned the tiny piece of tinder a darker, singed color, but the tinder did not ignite. Char cloth would probably have ignited. I guess I was pushing my luck.

Use a rag to rub the chocolate candy bar into the bottom of the soda can. Eventually you'll smooth the bottom of the can to a shiny, mirror-like finish. It takes at least an hour, so it's not easy, by any means. If you have some other abrasive substance, like an SOS pad, Ajax cleanser, or Comet, the process will go a lot faster. I've been told that toothpaste will work as well.

While a commercial mirror available at outdoor stores will work better, using a polished soda can will still work. Sometimes.

What other improvised reflector materials might be used other than the bottom of a soda can?

1. The inside of a shiny aluminum bowl.
2. The shiny bowl-like reflector found inside the bulb end of a flashlight.
3. A relatively wrinkle-free piece of tin foil and a bowl or ball to shape it. Obviously, the shiny side of the foil needs to be on the side where the tinder will be held at the focal point.

It's important to keep in mind that the focal point will be vary with bowl size. These homemade marginal reflectors must have the tiny piece of tinder at the exact focal point (or as close to it as you can get).

To find the focal point, take a tiny piece of paper about the size of a postage stamp and hold it where you think the focal point might be. Move the paper back and forth until you see the reflection on the paper reduce itself to a tiny dot of light. That tiny dot is where you need to hold the tinder.

Overall, this is an extremely difficult method.

BATTERY AND STEEL WOOL: This is a neat little method I stumbled across about twenty-five years ago. I was skeptical at best when I first heard of it but was pleasantly surprised to discover that not only does this method work, it's also easy to do, unlike some other methods I've described. In fact, I was successful on my very first attempt.

I held four C-cell batteries together in a series in my hands and touched about a 12-inch strand of steel wool to each battery. The steel wool ignited instantly, and I could have started a fire easily.

Virtually any type battery will work, but regular flashlight batteries are generally only 1.5 volts, so you might have to use several flashlight batteries held together in a series, end to end. A car battery, even a "dead" car battery, would light the steel wool in a heartbeat. Once the steel wool is ignited, use it to light your tinder. This is an "easy to do" method.

This method seems simple enough, but as usual, there are always some details that might not be readily apparent. For example, the strands of steel wool can't be too thick, nor can they be too tightly wound, or else they will act much like an electrical wire going to a lamp. The wool will simply conduct the electricity and drain the battery without igniting. The strands need to be loose.

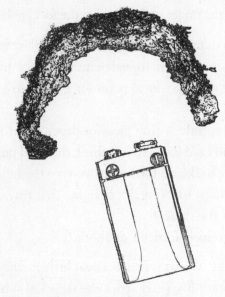

Setup for 9-volt battery and steel wool

A loose strand of steel wool, like tinder, allows air to get around its tiny threads, thus helping ignition. Whatever the scientific reason, ignition is more difficult if the strands are too tightly woven.

Also, the more voltage, the better chance of success. When I used the C-cell batteries, I was successful, but when I tried to use them a second time, I couldn't get the second batch to ignite as quickly because C-cells are only 1.5 volts. A single 9-volt battery like you use in smoke alarms is easier to use, higher in voltage, and the two terminals are conveniently on the same end of the battery.

In today's world, batteries are available from all sorts of devices you might have with you when unexpectedly stranded.

You can even use this method with a ball of paper held in your hand. Simply repeat the process above, but place the steel wool inside a ball of paper so that the

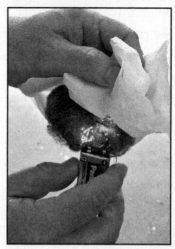

The battery will ignite the steel wool and the paper.

paper will ignite. The voltage will ignite the steel wool and the paper. Just take care not to hold on to the paper for too long!

PISTON: Sometimes referred to as a fire piston, this device consists of two pieces: the piston (or plunger) and a cylinder.

It works on the principle that when air is compressed, it heats

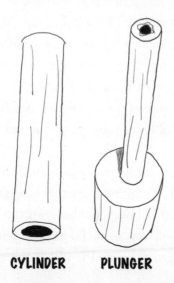

CYLINDER   PLUNGER

Piston kit

up. A tiny piece of tinder is placed inside the concave recess in the end of the plunger. The plunger is then inserted just inside the cylinder. At this point, the plunger is pushed down into the cylinder hard and fast. This creates heat (like a diesel engine) and ignites the tinder. Then you dump out the smoldering piece of tinder and blow on it to ignite your tinder ball.

The plunger must fit almost perfectly in the cylinder for this device to work. If the fit is even slightly loose, it either won't work at all, or it will require some thick lubricant or gasket to make the fit "tighter."

A fire piston is difficult—if not impossible—to make in the field on short notice. You could use bamboo for the cylinder, but the plunger would probably take a fair amount of tedious, smooth, and careful whittling.

If made in advance, the fire piston's main advantage is that it can be used for a lifetime, would never require lighter fluid, nor would you have to worry about the flint ever wearing out (since there isn't one). The fire piston is extremely durable and long lasting.

Portable Campfire: In rare situations, it might be convenient to have a quick-fired campfire, like a coffee can heater, that you can basically carry around with you. Most people use these little devices as heaters in deer stands during cold weather. As a portable, quick-start fire, they are hard to beat.

A portable campfire requires a metal can, approximately the size of a coffee can, a partial roll of toilet paper, and some rubbing alcohol to use as fuel.

Simply unroll enough paper from the toilet paper roll so that it will fit inside the coffee can. You can leave the cardboard tube where it is. Pour a few ounces of rubbing alcohol into the can, taking care to soak the paper on top well. Don't just pour it in the center where the cardboard tube is. Then light the toilet paper roll as you would a candle.

One word of caution: the portable campfire produces a flame

about two inches high, but it burns so purely that the flame is all but invisible. In daylight, you can barely see the flame at all, but trust me on this, it is still hot.

You can use the fuel as needed. A few ounces of rubbing alcohol in the bottom of the can will burn for fifteen to twenty minutes, perfect if you only need a quick warm up before moving on. Half a bottle of rubbing alcohol will literally burn for hours.

To extinguish the campfire, suffocate the flame with the coffee can lid or similar material.

A coffee can heater can be used

1. To quickly warm up while traveling and is easy to carry with you for next time.
2. To heat food like a stove or campfire.
3. As a heat source/starter to get an actual campfire going.
4. As a lantern.
5. As an evasion, as it is smokeless and virtually odorless, unlike a traditional campfire.

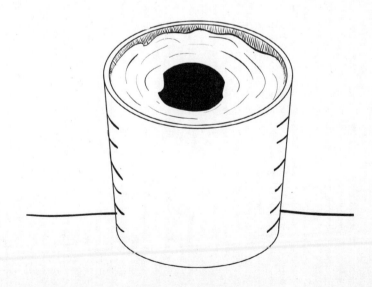

Portable campfire using coffee can and toilet paper

CHAPTER TWO
GATHERING FISH AND WATER RESOURCES

When you're starting a fire, the primitive and sometimes laborious methods found in chapter 1 can be pretty much avoided. A Bic lighter in your pocket simplifies a lot of things, doesn't it? Still, the information is good to know, especially if you're stranded unexpectedly.

Unfortunately, when it comes to gathering fish, there's not such a simple alternative. But by planning ahead, and thus having better equipment, virtually all of the gathering techniques in this chapter will still be as useful. They will just be much easier and greatly enhanced.

These are not traditional "sport fishing" methods. This is about "gathering" fish (as the chapter name implies) and other water resources. Sport fishing is fun, but it is a lot of work in some instances.

GATHERING FISH

These methods use as little work as possible. Natural, simple, and easy is definitely what we are shooting for here.

SHALLOW INLET POOL—Most anyone who has wandered around woods and streams has encountered a shallow inlet pool. It is a geographic condition that allows you to practically walk up and grab a few fish to eat.

Admittedly, this naturally occurring "trap" won't help you much if you are in the Mohave Desert where there are simply no streams, lakes, or ponds. But, in most of North America (and again, this book is written for Joe Average North American), there is some sort of creek, stream, pond, or lake within a mile or two.

Look for a spot where the main source of water has overflowed and filled a small pool. Most of us have seen these small pools just off the main body of water. Small fish are often stranded in the pool because the water level has dropped slightly and they can't get back out. This is the basic situation we are looking for in this natural fish trap. Cranes and other fish-eating birds look for these inlet pools because the small fish are easier to catch where they have less room to maneuver.

The small pool shouldn't be so large or deep that you can't catch (by spearing or netting, preferably) the small fish that have aimlessly wandered into it.

If the situation were perfect, the pool would be about 4 feet across and no more than about 8 inches deep. The "gate" into the pool should be only about a foot across. Of course, things are rarely perfect. A pool that's little larger or deeper may still work if you have a fairly good spear or net. We'll visit spears and nets later.

With a little digging, this topographical situation can sometimes be created on your own if it does not occur naturally.

If you find yourself in a situation where you plan to return to the location many times and use it as a continuing resource, then making the "gate" deeper will allow for larger fish. However, this is generally a trap for smaller fish.

Another variation is to drive sticks or pile rocks, boards, or whatever is available into the entrance or "gate" in a V shape. This helps to funnel the fish into the trap but will make it harder for them to find their way out once they are inside. With this V-shaped entrance set up, it will be less important to walk up from the gate side of the pool when checking the trap.

What about bait? It usually depends on the situation. This trap generally captures small fish—it works best on perch—in their natural comings and goings. They will readily swim into these small inlet pools, apparently not realizing there may be no getting out.

However, if you plan to use this trap repeatedly over a period of time, bait couldn't hurt. If you're not in an actual survival situation, small pieces of white bread will bring in the perch, and the perch might even attract larger predator fish, like bass. But if you *are* in a survival situation, eat the bread yourself and use wild bait.

Check any old, rotten stumps or logs nearby for beetles and grubs. If you can break open the rotten wood, you can literally pick these bugs up by the hundreds sometimes. Grasshoppers are good bait. Digging for worms is a lot of work, but if there is no other option, you might consider it. Pouring bleach into an earthworm hole will make them wiggle to surface, where you can pick it up. If you can spear a snake or a single small perch, chop it up and toss it in to use as bait.

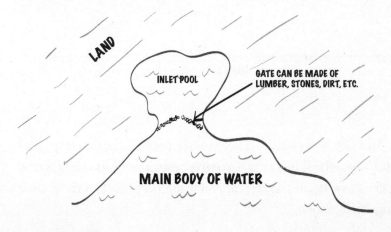

Shallow inlet pool

BANK VERSION: SHALLOW INLET POOL—If there is no naturally occurring inlet pool, you can create one by driving bamboo or other sticks into the mud to form a box on the bank. As with the diagram of the other trap, place a V-shaped funnel on the deep end to let the fish in easily and to make it harder for them to find their way out.

Obviously, the water cannot get deep instantly off the bank. You need to find a place where you can wade out at least a few feet in order to drive the stakes in the mud to form the trap.

This is more work than the naturally occurring inlet pool, but it does have an advantage. If the bamboo you are using is long enough, the deep end of the trap could be a little deeper, thus making it available to larger fish.

To lessen the labor of construction, use netting or some other material to reduce the amount of stakes you'll need to drive into the mud. The only thing that matters is that the fish can get in but not out. See drawing.

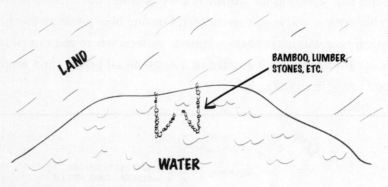

LAND

BAMBOO, LUMBER, STONES, ETC.

WATER

Bank version of inlet pool

SHALLOW STREAM TRAP—After seeing the two traps previously described, this trap is relatively obvious in its use by viewing the drawing. If the stream is not too deep, rocks can be used instead of bamboo.

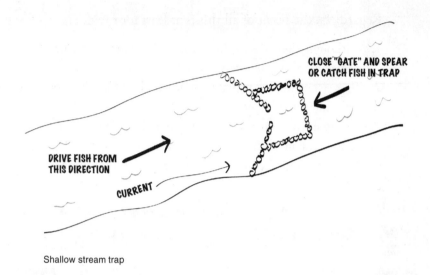

CLOSE "GATE" AND SPEAR
OR CATCH FISH IN TRAP

DRIVE FISH FROM
THIS DIRECTION

CURRENT

Shallow stream trap

MINNOW SEINES—A minnow seine is something you rarely see anymore. A minnow seine is a tightly woven net for catching minnows to use as bait. The net is usually about 3 to 4 feet wide and 15 to 20 feet long with floats attached to the top edge of the net and weights attached to the bottom edge. It has two poles attached to the ends that are each about 5 feet long.

The seine is used by two people who wade out into a water source with a gently sloping floor. The water shouldn't be more than 3 feet deep. You both place the bottom end of the seine down to the floor and walk to the shore. The seine will form a slight U behind you. Once you reach the bank, the net will be full of minnows.

Seines were popular through the 1960s but aren't so much anymore. There may be legal ramifications now that didn't exist then. Or perhaps we are all too affluent and just buy bait at the local bait shop on the rare occasions we go fishing. Whatever the reason, seines are just not as prevalent as they have been in the past, and many younger people have probably never seen one.

Regardless, the point of all this is at least four fold:

1. Although they are made to catch tiny bait fish, a minnow seine will also catch larger fish. '
2. Larger netting, if available, will let small fish through and only catch the larger ones.
3. In some survival situations, you may be able to improvise a crude version of this net.
4. It is a fairly quick and easy method of reaping fish resources.

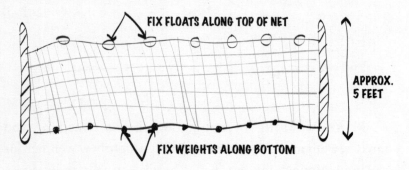

Minnow seine

HOLLOW LOG TRAP—This is another fish trap that doesn't require a lot of work, nor does it require hooks, weights, corks, or even bait. It does require that you find three items, which could probably be improvised or scrounged from a lot of different sources.

First, it takes a hollow log about three or four feet long. This log needs to have an inside diameter of at least four inches but not more than twelve inches. It also must be heavy or waterlogged enough that it won't float to the water's surface, but not so heavy that you can't carry it to the water. It doesn't necessarily need to be an actual log. Just about any hollow cylinder (an eight-inch diameter PVC pipe would be ideal) that is the same size would probably work fine, as long as it will sink readily to the bottom of the body of water.

Second, you will need something to plug one end of the log, like a rock wedged in the opening or a mesh net. You want something that will allow water to flow through the cylinder and still trap the larger fish you're trying to catch. Blocking one end will make it harder for fish to swim out the open end and will make it easier to pull the trap up more rapidly. See illustration.

Third, you will need a rope, cord, cable, wire, or something similar to tie to the open end of the log that will enable you to yank it up quickly when checking it.

These types of traps are predominantly used in the South to catch large catfish. They are occasionally used to catch other types of fish and sometimes turtles.

As usual, the details are important.

The log or cylinder must be at least 3 feet long—preferably 4 feet. The longer the length, the harder it will be for the fish to escape when you are hurriedly pulling up the open end. If your snare was only 2 feet long, more fish would swim out on the way up.

Fish won't be clamoring to be the first to get into the hollow log trap. It is one of those traps that needs to be left alone for a while, perhaps a full day. Why large catfish go into these traps in the first place is a mystery since the trap is not baited. Perhaps they're seeking some shelter. Regardless of the reason, the hollow log trap is effective and easy to construct.

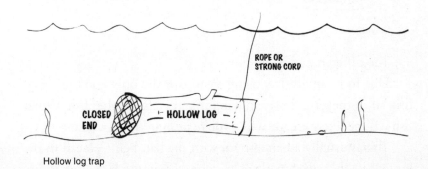

Hollow log trap

CRAYFISH TRAP—Crayfish are fresh water versions of shrimp, so if you like shrimp, you'll probably like crayfish or, as we call them in Texas, "crawfish."

The crayfish trap is a smaller version of the hollow log trap. It utilizes the same hollow cylinder, but in this case, it's usually just a tin can, preferably no smaller than a coffee can. You punch holes on all the sides and along the bottom of the tin can—the more holes the better. Attach a string to the open end of the can, just like in the hollow log trap. Lower the can in the water in the same manner as the hollow log trap and pull on the string quickly to retrieve the trap in the same way.

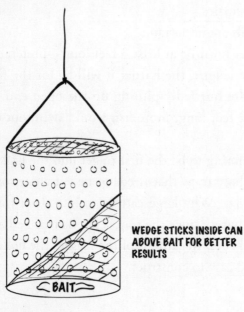

WEDGE STICKS INSIDE CAN
ABOVE BAIT FOR BETTER
RESULTS

BAIT

Crayfish trap

The differences are these.

Due to its small size, using a can is really only good for crayfish, since they are slower moving than perch or other fish. Other fish will be likely escape while you're pulling the can up.

This is usually a baited trap, with the bait being placed in the bottom of the can. Small sticks, wire, screen mesh, or something similar is wedged into the can just above the bait. The purpose of this is to make it more difficult for these shrimp-like critters to escape back through the sticks or wire when you go to retrieve the can. If available, a coil of screen wire inserted into the can creates a "snag" for crayfish claws and makes it more difficult for them to get out. This is basically a survival trap. You won't catch a lot of food in one of these. The crayfish would really have to be plentiful for you to be well fed.

Burlap Bag Crayfish Trap—If a burlap bag or similar material is available, this is a simple way to catch a few crayfish, emphasis on "few."

Find an area at the water's edge where the water is only about 4 inches deep for at least 3 or 4 feet out into the water. Lay the burlap bag flat into the water and let it saturate and settle to the bottom. If the water is wavy at all, you may have to lay a rock on the two outmost corners to make the bag stay put. Leave the bag alone for a few hours at least.

Eventually the crayfish will take shelter under the bag. There may be only a few or there may be fifty, depending on how plentiful they are in your particular spot.

When you are ready to check your trap, do two things.

First, pull the bag out of the water by dragging it along the bottom and then flick the bag 3 or 4 feet back out of the water. Next, turn your attention to the crayfish that are still in the water. Grab them using the net. They're pretty quick, so you will lose a lot of them if you have no net. Still, you'll be able to grab a few even using just your hands. Toss them back on the bag that you threw on shore.

Turn your attention back to the burlap bag and the crayfish you have just tossed onto it. You will find that the burlap has provided a "snag" for the crayfish claws and that there are at least a few stuck to the bottom of the burlap bag. This is why you *drag* the bag out rather than lifting it so that the crayfish won't have time to dislodge their claws. Again, you won't feed a big group with this trap.

FISHING POLE SEINE—This is another trap that will only capture a few small fish, but it works for you while you do something else. And it can be improvised out of nearly anything.

This seine requires a 12-foot piece of fairly rigid wire that can be bent into a 3-foot square. It is better if the wire is considerably heavier than coat hanger wire but still malleable using your hands. Once you've shaped your square, secure the two ends together by twisting or using duct tape. This must be a solid, secure connection at the corner.

Next, attach a cloth across the square fairly tightly. White cloth seems to work best, but use whatever you have available. You don't want much slack. If you have sewing materials available, sewing the cloth to the frame is perhaps the best way. However, in a survival situation, tying the cloth across the square might be possible if you have enough cordage.

Next, tie four equal lengths of cord, each about three feet long, to each of the four corners of the square. Then tie a single cord or rope to the four corner cords so that when you pull up on the single cord, all four corners of the square will come up levelly. This may take some trial and error.

At this point, you've pretty well done the hard part. The only other things you will need are (1) a traditional fishing pole, as long as it is solid and not bamboo. Bamboo will break too easily in this snare; (2) a Y-shaped stake to drive in the mud near the bank; and (3) a small stake with some cord to adjust the height.

Set the system as in the illustration to a depth of about four inches, six at the most. Place a small stone dead center in your square, place some bait there, and leave it be for a while.

When you can see the small fish swimming above the white cloth to get at the bait, pull up the net. This is why it is important that all four corners coming up at the same time. If your trap isn't level—say, one corner is much lower than the other three—the fish will escape in that direction.

Commercial models of this device are probably available, but I've never seen one. It is actually a minnow or small bait fish trap, but as with the minnow seine earlier, it can be used to catch larger fish.

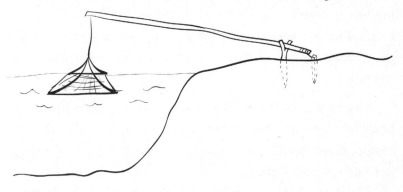

CONE TRAP—This is a basic fish trap that almost everyone on earth has seen at one time or another. It is basically a wire cylinder with a funnel in each end and bait in the center. The fish can get in, but not out.

Cone snares can be tiny, for minnows and the like. Or they can be made several feet long with large diameter funnels for much larger fish.

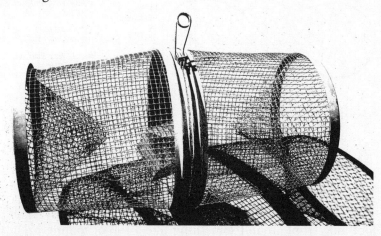

Cone trap with wire bait holder to lure fish in through the cones' openings.

If you have cordage and need to make do with primitive materials, a cone trap can be made from bamboo. It is time consuming, but not difficult.

All cone snares, regardless of size, all work basically the same way. Typically, the bait is simply tossed in the trap, allowing fish to nibble at it from outside the trap. Add a screen wire bait holder to the center of this trap to force the fish to swim inside the trap before they can get to the bait. This increases the take.

CLOVERLEAF FISH TRAP—This fish trap is absolutely the best I have ever seen for catching small fish. If there are fish to be caught, this trap will catch them by the hundreds. It is a "reaping the wild resources" item.

The cloverleaf trap is basically a cone trap on steroids. It works on the same basic principle but simply catches a lot more. It is made from hardware cloth or similar wire that is stiff enough to hold its own shape.

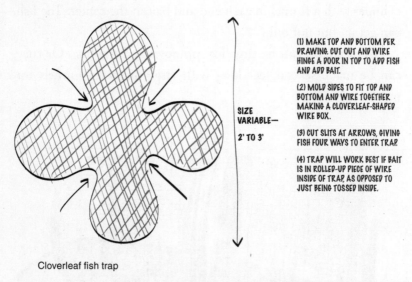

SIZE VARIABLE— 2' TO 3'

(1) MAKE TOP AND BOTTOM PER DRAWING. CUT OUT AND WIRE HINGE A DOOR IN TOP TO ADD FISH AND ADD BAIT.

(2) MOLD SIDES TO FIT TOP AND BOTTOM AND WIRE TOGETHER MAKING A CLOVERLEAF-SHAPED WIRE BOX.

(3) CUT SLITS AT ARROWS, GIVING FISH FOUR WAYS TO ENTER TRAP.

(4) TRAP WILL WORK BEST IF BAIT IS IN ROLLED-UP PIECE OF WIRE INSIDE OF TRAP AS OPPOSED TO JUST BEING TOSSED INSIDE.

Cloverleaf fish trap

Make the middle first. Bend the hardware cloth (at least a foot-long strip) around something like a roll of roofing paper to form the cloverleaf shape and wire the two ends together.

Next, cut two pieces of the hardware cloth to the cloverleaf shape to serve as the top and bottom. Wire them to the middle all around the edges.

Cut an opening from the top for a door. "Hinge" it with wire so you can open and shut it when you want.

Cut four slots for fish to enter as shown in the diagram. Push the sharp points of the wire inward so that the fish can swim into the trap easily but not the other way around.

This cloverleaf trap is easy to make and easy to use.

FISHING POLE SNARE—This device is a combination of fishing and snaring. It can be used in only limited situations, but it requires little in the way of equipment.

First, the situation. At times, you might face a scenario where the water is shallow enough (2 feet or less) and clear enough that you can see fish moving around slowly or perhaps just resting in place in the water, but the water is too deep or the fish have enough maneuverability, and you can't catch them by hand. You have no real fishing equipment or netting.

In this admittedly limited scenario, the fishing pole snare might come in handy.

You will need a basic fishing pole of almost any sort, like a solid tree limb. Anything will do. Ideally, a 6-foot long bamboo pole would be best since it is strong enough for this type of use and yet still flexible.

Second, you will need at least four feet—preferably five feet—of stranded copper lamp cord wire or something similar. If you cut the insulation away from the wire of almost any appliance (like a lamp), you will find tiny strands of copper wire woven together. Strip the insulation from the four-foot length of wire and separate the copper strands down to about fifteen or twenty strands. Twist the strands in your fingers so that they are "woven" into a single strand.

Form a tiny loop in one end. Run the other end through the tiny loop, forming a lasso. The diameter of the lasso is normally small, only slightly larger than the size fish you are seeing in the water.

Tie the other end of the wire to the end of your fishing pole. You now have a traditional fishing pole with line, except that you have a wire lasso on the end where you would normally find the weight and hook.

Instead of hooking a fish, the fishing pole snare works by the copper wire cutting into the fish just enough to give you time to flip it out onto the bank. In order to do this, you have to get the loop around the fish, which requires slow—very slow—non-threatening movements. Obviously, the longer the fish, the easier this will be.

If the fish are gently moving in one direction, you can place the loop in front of them and let one swim into it. They generally don't seem to be threatened by the wire loop. Perhaps it just looks like normal vegetation in the water to them.

This process works best if you can catch the fish with the snare just in front of their dorsal (top) fin but behind their side fins in the gill area. It works much better on catfish because (1) they have more prominent dorsal and pectoral fins; and (2) the snare loop will "hold" better because catfish don't have hard and slick scales like perch, allowing the wire to cut more easily into their softer bodies.

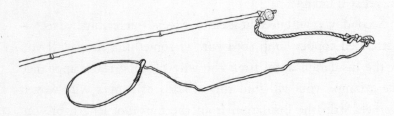

Fishing pole snare

IMPROVISED SPEARS—Many of the fish traps shown earlier will be much easier if you can harvest the fish with a spear instead of your bare hands.

A commercially made model is a typically a trident with each of the three metal spears being around three inches long. Generally, you buy the trident but have to supply your own wood pole. I haven't bought one lately, but I'd be surprised, even in today's world, if they were more than five dollars.

Like almost every method we've discussed about fish gathering, a commercially made model of this item will be better than a spear you make in the field, but you might find yourself in a situation where making your own is necessary.

Bamboo is easy to use in making improvised fishing spears, although almost anything could be used. Sharpen one end, and then, with the point of a knife, drill a tiny hole in the side and insert sliver of bamboo to form barb.

Or you can whittle a bamboo "arrowhead" and insert it in the blunt end of your bamboo. Unlike a bamboo barb, it will have to be glued in with tree resin, mud, modern glue, and so on. On the right, bamboo is sharpened and whittle into barbed shape.

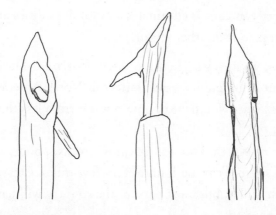

Improvised bamboo spear tips

OBTAINING WATER:

PUBLIC WATER RESOURCES—As long as we don't face a complete societal collapse, our public water resources will always be hard to beat.

First, water is extremely cheap from the tap. Even if you buy bottled water and don't drink from your public municipality, it is still relatively inexpensive.

Second, the use of public water resources eliminates everything else in this section about filtering, purifying, and avoiding contaminants. Anything going wrong with the public water supply and subsequent issuance of "boil water" notices is so rare in North America that it doesn't even warrant a second thought.

Third, even in the event of a catastrophic collapse of public services, it is very unlikely that such an event would happen so quickly that you didn't have time to store as much water as you want.

Having numerous empty containers around to store water in, if things begin to look shaky, could be a big plus. It's more likely that you'll have plenty of time to store water but not have anywhere near enough containers to store it in.

In other words, use commercially available water wherever and whenever you can. It eliminates a lot of difficulties and gives you more time to reap other resources.

RIVERS, STREAMS, LAKES, AND PONDS—Having said all that about using public water sources in North America, there may be times when you have to obtain water from less than desirable sources.

In most of North America, streams, creeks, ponds, lakes, or other water sources can be found every few miles. Okay, maybe not in Death Valley, but most parts of the country will have water somewhere nearby.

Think about it. Wherever you live or happen to be, how far

would it be to the nearest source of water? Even the smallest stream or creek? Most large cities will have some sort of creek or river running through them. In rural areas, like where I live in Texas, there is a stock pond, creek, or some water source within a mile of nearly anywhere.

Have these sources in mind ahead of time. It doesn't take a lot of water to sustain you or even a small party. But water is a must. You can do without food for quite a while, but dehydration begins in two or three days, even under ideal circumstances like moderate or cool weather with little or no exertion. Exerting yourself in hot weather would push this envelope up much quicker.

Obtaining Water with Solar Still—If public water is no longer available, and you are in one of those rare areas where there simply is not a creek, stream, river, or other "wild" water resource, a solar still will usually produce enough water for you to survive—again, emphasis on "survive."

Solar stills will not produce abundant amounts of water, but they will almost always work, even in a desert.

I first saw this device around 1960 or so. It may be much older than that, and I have no idea who invented it originally. The technique has become fairly well known over the years.

All you need to build a solar still are two common items: a thin piece of plastic (poly) that is about five feet square. The exact size doesn't matter. This is the type of plastic that might be wrapped around your clothes when they come back from the cleaners or the thin plastic sheeting that painters sometimes use for drop cloths. The other item is a cup or container of some sort to collect the water. Something the size of a large coffee cup or so is about right.

Select a site for the solar still in the lowest possible (and still reasonable) elevation level. The lower the elevation, the greater the likelihood of there being moisture in the soil. A creek bed is ideal. Even if the creek is dry, there will often be moisture a few inches under the soil. Naturally, use common sense. There are always exceptions to every general rule.

The premise of the solar still is that the moisture in the freshly dug soil will evaporate under the plastic, and then condense on the under side of the plastic sheeting. The water will then trickle down the underside of the plastic, and drip off at the lowest point (directly over the cup).

1. Dig a circular hole three or four feet in diameter and about a foot deep in the center.
2. Place the cup in the bottom of the hole as close to dead center as you can.
3. Stretch the plastic sheeting relatively tightly across the top of the hole and weigh down the edges with stones. Place a small stone on the plastic directly over the cup.

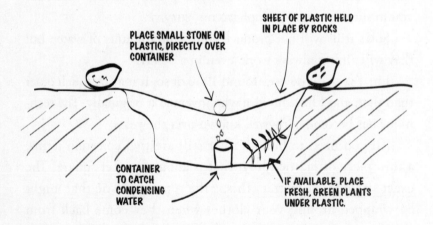

I'm told (and I hope never to find out from practical experience) that the solar still will even work in relatively dry desert areas. You probably won't get a lot of water, but even a little water beats no water by a long shot.

Obviously, in areas where the soil is not parched of water, the solar still works exceptionally better.

Move the still each day as the moisture in the soil in any particular spot will be depleted.

Variation: If green vegetation is available, even a cactus in the desert, cut some of that vegetation and toss it into the still under the plastic. Just like the soil, the vegetation will give up its moisture into the air, and collect on the underside of the plastic. This variant might be especially helpful in desert areas.

OBTAINING RAIN WATER—Obtaining rain water is not quite as simple as it might sound.

Clearly, it needs to rain, and you must have a container, or multiple containers, to catch the rain. But, more than that, a tarp or a relatively large piece of plastic—like one used in the solar still—can be used to vastly multiply the amount of rain water gathered.

(1) STRETCH OUT TARP OR PLASTIC OVER GROUND WITH A SLIGHT INCLINE

(2) STAKE OFF CORNERS SO THAT RAIN WATER FLOWS OFF TARP INTO ONE SPOT

(3) DIG HOLE, IF NECESSARY, FOR COLLECTION BUCKET.

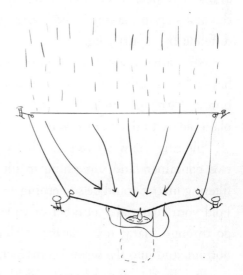

Obtaining rain water using a tarp

Consider these scenarios:

Scenario 1: Mother Nature provides a good soaking—an inch of rain over a period of about an hour. However, the only container you have is a 10-gallon plastic bucket. If you put the bucket out in the rain for the entire hour, you will have an inch of water in the bottom of the bucket. Not much.

Scenario 2: Mother Nature provides the same inch of rain, and you have the same 10-gallon plastic bucket. But this time, you also have a 10-foot-square plastic tarp. By stretching the plastic out so that the entire surface of it catches the rain, and by using gravity so that all the water flows off the tarp to one spot (the bucket), you can overflow the 10-gallon bucket several times over.

I call it the "gutter" principle. I'm sure you've noticed water literally flooding out of a gutter on a building when it is only lightly raining. It is the same principle.

FILTERING WATER:

For a practical matter, any water obtained outside of commercially available sources, needs to be filtered. Remember, filtering is only the first step in making "wild" water good enough to drink. It is different from purifying.

No matter how clean any stream or river looks, it is certain to have a lot of things in it that you don't want to drink. Even the purest of streams will have fish or animal waste, plant matter, and plain old dirt mixed in the water.

Filtering the water can be relatively easy, assuming you have two containers and something to filter the water through. The filtering matter could be something as simple as a shirt or a towel. Fold your material a number of times so that the water has to go through many, many layers of cloth before it comes out the bottom, and into the second container.

Ideally, the filter needs to be thick enough that it takes a while for the water to trickle through, as opposed to a simple, single-layered towel that the water will flow through almost nonstop.

Again, like the source of water, a commercially available filter bought ahead of time can save a lot of grief if you buy plenty of extra filter pads. But if you have to make one on your own, a fair "country boy" filter can be made by filling a container with alternating layers of sand, vegetation, and ash (from your campfire). The hole in the bottom of your container needs to be only penny sized. A two-liter plastic Coke bottle would work. Cut out the large end and use as in diagram.

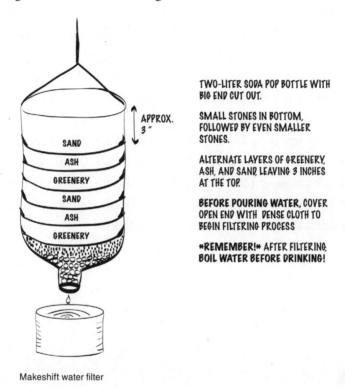

APPROX. 3"

SAND

ASH

GREENERY

SAND

ASH

GREENERY

TWO-LITER SODA POP BOTTLE WITH BIG END CUT OUT.

SMALL STONES IN BOTTOM, FOLLOWED BY EVEN SMALLER STONES.

ALTERNATE LAYERS OF GREENERY, ASH, AND SAND, LEAVING 3 INCHES AT THE TOP.

BEFORE POURING WATER, COVER OPEN END WITH DENSE CLOTH TO BEGIN FILTERING PROCESS

REMEMBER! AFTER FILTERING, BOIL WATER BEFORE DRINKING!

Makeshift water filter

Purifying Water:

Now that you have filtered water that is pretty much free of trash particles, the next step is to purify it.

Your filtered water may look good and clean already, but even the cleanest mountain stream will have bacteria or water-borne parasites. The price of getting sick with several days of diarrhea, or possibly even death, is too great to take a chance.

There are two general methods for purifying water, but I would only use one, and I don't recommend the other.

By far, the most sure fire method is to simply boil the water. Bring the water to a boil and allow it to boil vigorously for at least five minutes. Boiling the water leaves it with a "flat" taste when you drink it, but that is a small price to pay. This flat taste can be softened somewhat by pouring the water back and forth from one container to another.

The other method is chemical treatment. There are numerous brands of water purification tablets in sporting goods stores that you can buy before a trip, but they only work some of the time. There is even a list of various bacteria and viruses on the package that the product will not eliminate. I don't recommend chemical tablets unless it's a last resort. Household bleach can also be used, but I don't recommend this method either. But if you're in a pinch, ten drops of bleach per gallon is the correct ratio. There is just something about putting these chemicals into water that I plan to drink that I can't quite make myself do.

CHAPTER THREE
SNARES, TRAPS, AND IMPROVISED HUNTING GEAR

I like snares for a myriad of reasons.

First, snaring is something of a lost art in North America, though not in other parts of the world, especially Africa. Like silencers for firearms, most people in North America have probably never seen one and would be relatively unsure of how they work.

Second, when I first started toying with snares about thirty years ago, I felt they were probably something that looked good on a TV show or movie but probably didn't work all that well in the real world. I was wrong. They work extremely well.

Third, they are the essence of simplicity: cheap to make, easily carried, and difficult to spot once set.

Finally, just like the fish traps earlier, these snares work for you while you are doing something else. They are primitive but chillingly effective.

For the purposes of this book, we will go over basic snaring. There are literally hundreds of different possible snare sets, and most of those have variations. For a lengthier description of snaring, see *Into The Primitive—Advanced Trapping Techniques* published by yours truly back in 1989.

SQUIRREL SNARE—The first and most simple snare we will look at is generally referred to as a squirrel snare by most people.

First, use wire for the snare loop itself. I've seen numerous sources that say to use various types of cords and string, and they might work in extremely limited scenarios. But generally, cord or string aren't effective. Use wire.

Wire works better for a lot of reasons.

1. When the snare lasso tightens around the animal, the wire lasso tends to cut into the animal and will not loosen, thus trapping or killing the prey.
2. Wire will generally hold the lasso upright and open by itself when it is set and will require little or no support from surrounding vines or grass.
3. Animals don't seem to be alarmed by wire snare loops. Perhaps wire has less of an odor than string, or perhaps the wire blends in to nearby grass or vegetation.
4. The type of wire we are discussing has "memory" that string does not. This "memory" will help the lasso snap shut once tripped.
5. Once caught, the animal will have a harder time chewing through in the coil—if it's able to get his teeth on the lasso at all.

For a squirrel snare, or virtually any small animal snare, lamp cord wire (or the electrical cord of almost any household appliance) is hard to beat. You'll probably be able to make several of these snares from one lamp cord wire. An old extension cord works fine. You can use almost any type of wire that has these tiny copper wires inside.

Peel the rubberlike insulation off the wire, leaving only the copper wire. Notice that this type of wire is not a single solid wire. It's actually composed of many hair-sized threads of copper wire that are twisted together as one inside the insulation. Use about twenty-five or so of these hair-sized threads of copper wire and twist them together as one. The length should be about sixteen inches or so.

Once you have the wire, simply create a lasso on one end and a small loop on the other end to anchor the snare.

The size of the lasso loop for squirrels is about two inches in diameter.

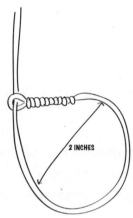

2 INCHES

Squirrel snare lasso

Once you've made the snare, setting this trap is relatively easy. Find or cut some poles about 2 inches in diameter and about 8 feet long. These will be used to lean up against trees in an area where you see squirrels. Squirrels will see these as convenient climbing poles to get up into the trees and will start using them almost immediately.

Attach the snare about half way (or a little more) up the pole. Once a squirrel's head or middle area is ensnared in the loop, they will generally fall off the pole while struggling against the wire snare. You will normally find them suspended in the air below the pole. This type of snare should be checked fairly frequently, quietly and from a distance, if possible.

Obviously, squirrel snares are situation oriented. They will only be worth your time and effort in an area where squirrels are fairly plentiful. If you sit down and remain quiet in a potential

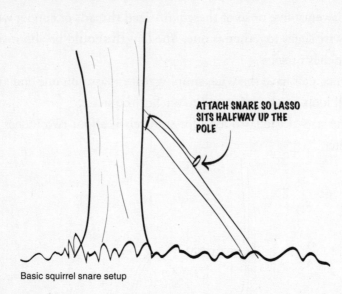

ATTACH SNARE SO LASSO
SITS HALFWAY UP THE
POLE

Basic squirrel snare setup

area for fifteen or twenty minutes and still don't see several squirrels sticking their noses out, you probably haven't found a good spot. Tree-lined creeks that are in otherwise open country are usually a good choice.

The following refinement takes advantage of the "memory" of the appliance wire we are using.

Form the loop for the snare the same way you would for the squirrel snare above, except this time, narrow the lasso size by forming it to point A in the drawing. The wire will tend to keep shape and form in which you bend it.

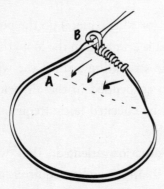

Squirrel snare lasso "memory" variation

Next, place a small bump in the wire at point B, which is just inside the lasso, and gently pull the loop back to point B and let it catch and rest on the bump you have made.

Now, the situation you have created with the snare is that with barely a jiggle, the wire loop wants to (and will) snap back to point A.

This seems like a tiny, insignificant change, but it will do two important things. (1) It helps the snare "snap shut" around the animal as it goes through it; and (2) if you use a triggered spring pole (discussed in the next section), this refinement insures that the trigger will be tripped.

Basic Spring Pole Snare—In the squirrel snare scenario, the squirrel ends up suspended in the air below the pole, and even if it's still alive, the squirrel has a hard time grabbing hold of anything in order to free itself.

A spring pole accomplishes the same thing, but it uses a different method to hold the struggling animal.

The wire snare loop itself is made exactly the same way. The use of the "wire memory" refinement would be the same, if used. Adjust the thickness of the wire and the size of the loop for whatever prey you intend to catch, but other than that, the actual snare lasso itself is the same.

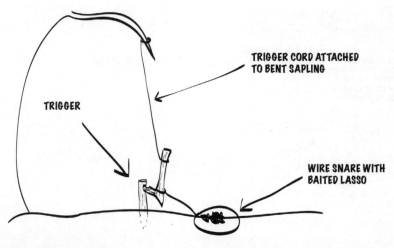

TRIGGER CORD ATTACHED TO BENT SAPLING

TRIGGER

WIRE SNARE WITH BAITED LASSO

Basic spring pole snare setup

The difference here is in the use of a bent sapling (spring pole) and a trigger to jerk the lasso tightly around the animal instead of letting the animal pull the snare tight around itself. You can use trot line cord (or almost anything) to attach the wire lasso to the spring pole.

The cord from the trigger is bent over the sapling (above, out of picture) that keeps line taut. If trigger is merely jiggled, trigger will release, and the spring pole will snap upward.

Logs or brush are normally used in such a way that the only convenient path to the bait is through the loop. If not baited, snares can be set in rabbit runs or trails or in entrances to den holes and in openings under fences. Any place where it is evident that the animal is coming and going frequently.

What if there is no convenient sapling to use as a spring pole? Sometimes you can use an overhanging limb and attach a weight to the other end. When the trigger is tripped, the weight goes down on one side of the limb, pulling upward the snare on the trigger side of the limb. Same principle. You will just be using a falling weight instead of the jerking motion of a spring pole.

ADDITIONAL SNARES

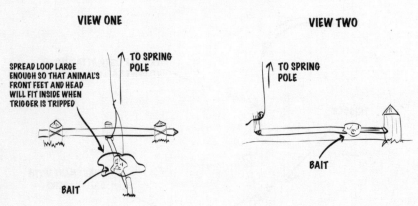

VIEW ONE

SPREAD LOOP LARGE ENOUGH SO THAT ANIMAL'S FRONT FEET AND HEAD WILL FIT INSIDE WHEN TRIGGER IS TRIPPED

TO SPRING POLE

BAIT

VIEW TWO

TO SPRING POLE

BAIT

DOUBLE SNARE VARIATIONS

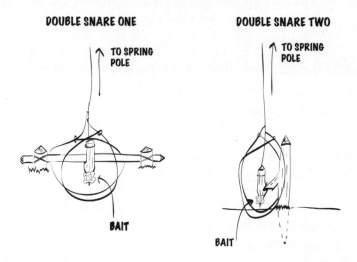

DOUBLE SNARE ONE

TO SPRING POLE

BAIT

DOUBLE SNARE TWO

TO SPRING POLE

BAIT

LARGE ANIMAL SNARE—The basic ideas behind large animal snares (to catch deer, for example) are pretty much the same, but they are a little different in design, use, and method of setting:

1. You would not use stranded wire on a large animal snare as we have done on the small snares described earlier. For large snares, it's best to use cable, which technically *is* stranded wire, but not in the sense that we have discussed earlier. The appliance wire we were using for the small snares will unravel under stress much faster than cable. Cable of ⅛-inch weight, or some equally heavy gauge single wire, is necessary for large animals.
2. A slack stopper mechanism and a loop stop are generally used but aren't absolutely necessary.
3. Large animal snares aren't usually secured to the ground by a stake, spring pole, or the like. They are almost always weighted with an "anchor" that the animal will be able to drag for a while before tiring.
4. Large animal snares are rarely, if ever, baited. They take advantage of game trails and the animals' natural pathways.

5. Unlike the small snares, which will pretty much hold themselves upright and open by themselves, large animal snares are heavier and must be held in position with string (or even grass).

Like virtually everything in this book, a large animal snare is situation oriented. They are only worth your effort if you are in an area with a lot of game. Since they are not baited traps, it is imperative that you set these snares in areas where large numbers of animals are coming and going.

To make the deer snare, you will need

1. About 15 feet or so of ¹⁄₁₆ to ¼-inch cable or other heavy, single-gauge wire that a deer will unlikely break.
2. 3 cable clamps
3. A drag weight of some sort, 20 to 30 pounds.
4. A small, flat piece of metal about 1 x 1½ inches with holes on each half, slightly larger than your cable size.

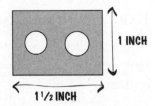

Before we actually get down to making the snare, let's talk about deer habits in the wild. Then the logic and method of deer snaring will make more sense.

First, if you have ever observed deer in the woods for any length of time, you will have noticed at least a couple of things. First, they tend to follow the same routes through wooded areas, creating trails that are visible to the hunter; and second, they tend to lower their heads to shoulder height as they push their way through a patch of tall grass.

As with any general rule, there are always exceptions. In a mature forest, where there is little or no underbrush, deer may move around in a more aimless, haphazard fashion. But, even then, there will be areas where deer trails will develop. The trails may be near where their path crosses a road or where they go to and from water.

Look for a spot on the deer trail where there is some tall grass or light brush on each side of the trail. The tall grass will be used to hold up (and camouflage) the snare.

Now that you have the site picked out, the making of the deer snare itself is relatively easy.

Take the 15-foot length of cable and loop the small piece of metal on one end using one of the cable clamps. Run the other end of the cable through the second hole of the small metal piece, thus forming a lasso.

The only purpose for the metal "slack stopper" is just that. Once the deer snugs the lasso up tight by walking through it, the metal piece (as opposed to just a lasso, as in the smaller snares) will prevent much slack from developing and keep it snugged up tight.

Next, use one of the other clamps by attaching it about 18 inches or so down the line from the slack stopper. The purpose of this is to simply keep the lasso from closing down to such a small loop that it will strangle the deer. You want your deer to still be alive when you find it.

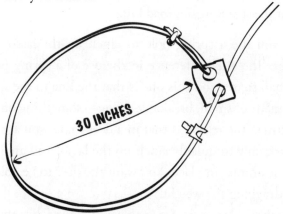

Large animal snare lasso with cable clamps

The correct diameter of the lasso for deer is about 30 inches, with the center of the lasso set at about belt-buckle height. Depending on how you attach the other end to the 20 or 30 pound anchor for the deer to drag around, you might not need the third cable clamp.

By now, the theory behind the deer snare is probably clear. This is what you hope to achieve:

1. The deer gets his head inside the cable snare in the process of pushing his way through some light brush or tall weeds.
2. As he walks a few steps, the snare cinches up tighter around his neck. The anchor weight on the other end of the snare cinches up the snare completely.
3. The cable clamp prevents the snare from getting so tight that the deer strangles to death. The slack stopper does the opposite, preventing the lasso from becoming loose. If you don't use a stop, the deer may die. The idea is fresh meat, not road kill.
4. The weight allows the deer to move around to some degree, helping him stay relatively calm. The weight also leaves a handy drag trail to follow and keeps the deer from getting too far away. You should be able to find the deer easily and dispatch it quickly. If you try to anchor the deer to the spot, instead of using a weight, it will almost certainly die pulling at the snare. Again, road kill.

Can you use a spring pole to cinch up the lasso on a deer snare? Yes. The only difference in the use of a spring pole in the earlier small snares and this one is that the line to the spring pole must be made of small, breakable string—something on the order of kite string. The reason is that in a deer snare, you are using the spring pole only to quickly cinch up the lasso. You are not trying to hold the animal in place. You want the deer to be able to move around, dragging the weight.

Does the cable in a deer snare have "memory" like the stranded copper wire in the smaller snares? No.

HAVAHART TYPE TRAPS—Most people have seen, or at least heard of, the old Havahart trap. It is basically a wire trap that is open at one end (some models are open at both ends) with a bait tray in the center.

When the animal comes in and jiggles the bait tray slightly, the end(s) snap shut, trapping the animal without killing it. These kind of traps allow you to release unwanted prey (like your neighbor's cat) unharmed, hence the name Havahart.

These traps have only limited use for either survival or reaping wild resources. Squirrels and the like are about the only edible creatures the Havahart would likely catch.

Havahart trap—Adding a metal tray to the bottom will prevent captured animals from hooking their claws into the wire floor of the trap and forcing their way out, damaging the trap.

TRADITIONAL SPRING TRAPS—For our purposes, the traditional spring trap would have limited use. Placing one at the entrance hole to a rabbit den or in the middle of a rabbit run might be one option.

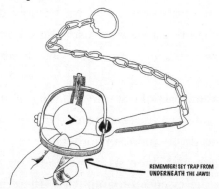

REMEMBER! SET TRAP FROM UNDERNEATH THE JAWS!

Traditional spring trap

When setting a spring trap, flip the snap bar opposite the trigger out of the way, and set the trap from *under* the jaws. (It bugs me when I see "experts" set a spring trap from above, with their fingers in between the jaws of the trap.)

WILD PIG TRAPS—Pig traps have become more prevalent in many parts of the country in the last twenty years as a result of the explosion in the population of wild pigs.

Wild pig traps are like Havahart traps, only they are a hundred times bigger and are made out of heavy gauge wire that the pigs can't break. These are definitely "reaping wild resources" traps. Just one of these traps can substantially supplement the family table if you have access to an area with wild pigs.

In rural Eastern Texas, where I live, I have seen one wild pig in the last ten years. It was near the side of a highway while I was driving to work. By far, I have seen more deer while out driving. Generally speaking, neither deer nor wild pigs are seen very often around here.

However, wild pigs are plentiful enough that they are a literal nuisance to people with pastureland. The pigs root up the land, creating huge holes that could almost swallow a pickup. Wild pigs aren't seen much, being mostly nocturnal, but they are there.

My brother and his neighbor started using a wild pig trap, and in the space of a little over a year, they caught over a hundred wild pigs. Of course, some were just piglets, but more than half were full grown. That's a lot of meat on the table for little effort.

By far, the hardest part of trapping wild pigs is the butchering and processing. Given the access and the trap, one of these devices can help feed you and many others.

Various triggers and door slam methods are used. This small pig trap is the essence of simplicity. There is a slot on each side that the door slides up and down within. A pin holds the door up and is connected to a wire running across the trap in the back. When the pig bumps this cross wire in the back of the trap (where the bait is) the pins are pulled out, and the door falls. My brother and his neighbor can catch a half a dozen pigs with a similar trap in a matter of weeks.

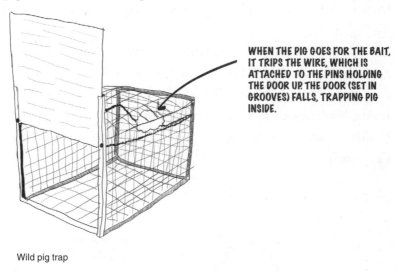

WHEN THE PIG GOES FOR THE BAIT, IT TRIPS THE WIRE, WHICH IS ATTACHED TO THE PINS HOLDING THE DOOR UP. THE DOOR (SET IN GROOVES) FALLS, TRAPPING PIG INSIDE.

Wild pig trap

Blowguns—A blowgun is strictly a survival item. It might help you stay alive by killing a few small birds, but that's about all. A blowgun won't do a lot of good in reaping wild resources except in these tiny amounts, unless, of course, you are an expert in utilization of poisons that will bring down larger game without tainting the meat. Some Native American tribes use this method to get monkey-sized game, but I would be reluctant to experiment. The down side is too great.

Having said all that, however, the upside is that a blowgun is easy to make. The parts can generally be scrounged from a wrecked car or downed aircraft if you are ever actually stranded in a remote area with little or no food or gear. And there are almost always small birds around, even in remote, desolate areas.

The homemade model I will describe can speedily fire a dart 20 yards or more with greater accuracy than one would think if they have never seen or used one. And, I confess, a blowgun is just kind of fun to mess around with too.

There are at least two kinds of blowguns that are relatively easy to make and use from improvised materials. The first is made from modern (non-jungle) type materials one could obtain from disabled cars or planes or from garage-type junk around the house.

The hollow tube is, of course, the most critical. Longer is generally better, but 30 inches long or so will do if you can't find anything longer. An ideal length would be 4 to 5 feet. The inside diameter of the tube isn't all that important. About a ½-inch inside diameter would be ideal, but you can use larger in a pinch.

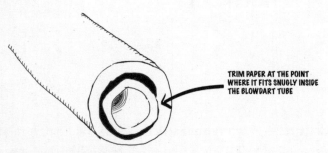

TRIM PAPER AT THE POINT WHERE IT FITS SNUGLY INSIDE THE BLOWDART TUBE

Blowgun tube with loaded dart

Tubing is everywhere in downed aircraft or wrecked cars. In cars, for example, there are fuel lines, brake lines, air conditioning tubing, and so on. The same is true for a fallen aircraft. The hardest part might be tearing the tubing out of the vehicle without bending it, all while keeping each end of the tube somewhat smooth, and emptying out the contents (brake fluid, for example).

The dart itself is made from paper rolled into a cone. For greatest power and accuracy, the paper cone needs to be torn off at the point that it fits exactly the inside diameter of whatever tubing you are using.

Last, the dart must be fitted with a nail-like tip. This can be taped into the cone or cemented with glue, if these modern materials are available. It not, use plant resin or tree sap. Slash a tree and let the sap flow. Nearly any tree sap is sticky, although sweet gum is ideal. Regardless, it won't take much sap for our purposes.

DART TIP IS A SMALL FINISH NAIL, NOT SHARPENED ANY MORE THAN IT CAME FROM THE LUMBER YARD

Blowgun dart made from rolled paper and a nail

Closeup impact of a blowgun dart. The unsharpened nail was buried approximately ½ inch. Blowguns are suitable for small, easily killed, sparrow-sized birds.

The second type of blowgun is only slightly different but is considerably more trouble to make. This blowgun is made from natural materials in the wild.

For the tube, you need to find some bamboo. Again, 3 feet or longer would be ideal. Using bamboo tubing can be tricky for several reasons:

- The inside diameter of the tube is inconsistent.
- The joints of bamboo are solid and have to be punched out from the end with a smaller shaft of wood
- Due to the inconsistent inside diameter of bamboo (or any natural material), a different type of dart must be used.

Still, the principle is the same as the first blowgun. The dart for a bamboo blowgun is a solid stick sharpened on one end. It is about the diameter of a wire coat hanger.

Glue some puffy material, like the down of a thistle, on the back end of the dart, so when you blow into the bamboo tubing, the down will fill up the inside diameter of the bamboo, propelling the dart out the other end.

SLINGS—I know I sound like a broken record, but slings are like everything else in this book—situation oriented.

Like the blowguns above, the sling (with practice) might enable you to take out a rabbit or ground squirrel, if you find yourself in an area that is practically overrun with such critters. But generally speaking, the sling is too primitive and inaccurate a weapon to reap large amounts of wild resources.

For most of us Joe Average North Americans, our time would be better spent elsewhere (like in setting up fish traps) in most situations.

Again, the situation you find yourself in determines what you need to do. However, assuming a sling would help you, it is an easily made, basic, and primitive item.

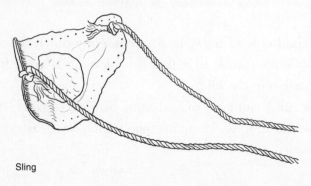

Sling

A sling is basically two strings, each about 3 feet long, with a leather-like pouch in the center. One of the strings has a loop to fit around your index finger. The other string is simply held in the same hand. The projectile (rock) is put in the pouch, twirled for momentum, and then released.

People usually make two common mistakes: first, they try to use small stones for ammunition; and second, they try to fire their ammunition with the speed of a bullet.

Larger, rounded stones have more impact damage, even though they travel much slower. Use ammo that is golf ball–sized at least. And don't try to fling anything at a your target with lightning speed. It's just like what your Little League coach told you when you were a kid swinging the bat at a baseball. Don't try to kill it—a smooth swing is more accurate.

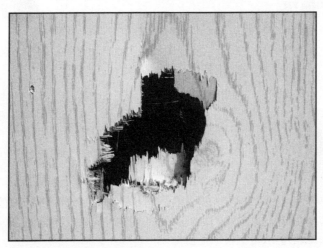

Impact of sling on plywood paneling

SLINGSHOTS—Everyone on the planet knows what a slingshot is and how it is used, so we won't waste a lot of time on them. But given a survival situation, knowing how to make a slingshot could be of some use.

The hardest component to find will be the elastic. Almost nothing works better than large rubber bands—the kind you would find in an office. Use 8 or 10 on each side of the fork. Regardless of what you might have read in survival articles, the elastic in your underwear does not work well for this. (Trust me on this, but don't ask how I know.)

What about ammo? Ball bearings, marbles, or round stones would be superior ammo in both accuracy and projectile speed. But even inadequate ammo (like the nut off a bolt, which isn't even round) will do the trick for small birds, maybe even rabbits, which is all a slingshot is good for anyway.

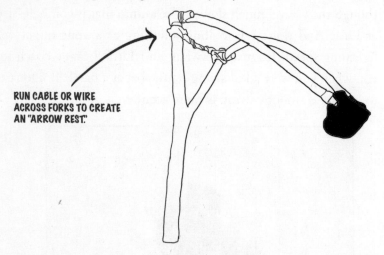

RUN CABLE OR WIRE
ACROSS FORKS TO CREATE
AN "ARROW REST."

Sling shot with arrow rest variation. Original slingshot used medical tubing (available at any pharmacy) for elastic and a tree branch for fork.

Variation: It is possible to use this same slingshot as a bow, if you have something to run across the forks, like a piece of snare wire, to create a "rest" for the arrow.

When I've used makeshift arrows (described later in this chapter) I have managed come within a couple of inches of my intended target, nearly fifteen yards away—more than close enough to hit a rabbit.

This improvised bow and arrow is relatively powerful as survival items go.

Closeup impact of a slingshot, using a nut from a bolt as projectile.

Using the same arrow discussed on page 75 with the slingshot "bow" variation. Accurate within a couple of inches.

BOLA—There are probably variations all over the world of the throwing weapon called a bola.

It is basically three (sometimes more) weights tied to three short lengths of rope. Twirled like a sling and then thrown, the three weights will separate in flight, cutting a larger swath through the air than a single stone. Thus, you are more likely to hit the target. When one of the weights (or ropes) strikes the target, it brings the wrapping action of the other ropes and the impact of the other weights into play.

We are all probably most familiar with the films of South American gauchos using the bola much like a North American cowboy uses his rope. The difference, of course, is that the North American cowboy holds onto one end of the rope while lassoing the cattle, whereas the gaucho throws the bola, letting it wrap up around the legs of the calf.

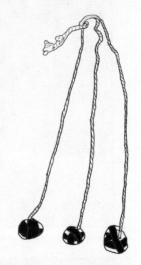

The bola wouldn't be of much use unless you find yourself in an unusual situation, but it never hurts to know the technique. After all, a successful throw of a bola will cut a large swath through a dense flock of flying birds, knocking down several, much like a shotgun.

Bola

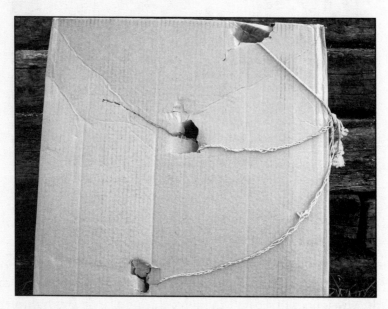

Impact of homemade bola into cardboard box. Most useful in rare instances of finding a flock of birds. A survival item only.

BOW AND ARROW—All of us Joe Average North Americans probably have a little spot of admiration in the back of our brains somewhere for the Native Americans who used the bow and arrow as an effective hunting weapon for hundreds (perhaps thousands) of years. Not only did they survive, but they *thrived*, eventually covering and populating the entire continent.

Nonetheless, for most of us Joe Average North Americans, trying to provide food for ourselves and our loved ones even with modern, high-tech archery equipment would be extremely difficult unless you happened to be in an area that was literally teeming with game.

Generally speaking, fish traps and other water resources will provide much more protein with a lot less work. However, in some survival circumstances, primitive bows and arrows could be of some use. For example, if you were stranded in an area where there are *lots* of small game, like rabbits or prairie dogs, a bow could be a great help.

In areas of west and southwest Texas, much of the desert is heavily populated with jack rabbits. I have personally walked up to within a few feet of these long-eared hares in the deserts of Big Bend National Park. They will stay very still (perhaps thinking you do not see them?) until you get to within a few feet. At times, it almost seems like you have to elbow them out of the way to walk, there are so many. Only in a situation similar to this one would it be worth the effort to make primitive archery equipment, because it does take some time and resources to make the gear.

Also, forget deer and other big game with primitive equipment. Stick with the rabbits and like fare.

Having prefaced the primitive bow and arrow with all that negativism, here are the basics:

Making a primitive bow for small game is one of those things where shorter really is better than longer for one basic reason. When having to gather the materials in the wild, it is simply much easier to find "springy" tree limbs or saplings that are 3 feet long than it is to find them 5 feet long. Also, the longer the bow is, the more receptive it is to breaking.

For the bow, the type of wood to use would vary from area to area. Different bow makers have touted yew, *bois d'arc*, cherry, oak, and many other types of wood.

But more important than what kind of wood you choose is its "springiness" once it's strung. Some species of wood when bent slightly (like a bow) will stay that way and not snap back to their original form when released. The bow, obviously, must have this "snap back" quality.

In some wood species, a bow will have this quality only when the wood is dry, and others only when green.

Finding straight limbs of the appropriate size is often difficult. The arrows for these relatively short survival bows are not much more than two feet long. The shorter they are, the easier it will be to find straight material. The longer they are, the harder they will be to find.

Cutting short saplings is often the only answer. In essence, you will be using the trunks of small trees rather than limbs.

If bamboo is available, it can be used with both advantages and disadvantages. The advantages:

1. You can almost always find it appropriate diameter of about ⅜ inch.
2. Bamboo is easy to notch (nock) on the back end for the string because it is hollow.
3. It is easier to attach whatever you are using for the arrowhead to bamboo for the same reason.

The two disadvantages:

1. Because it is hollow, bamboo is lighter and will have slightly less impact energy.
2. The bumps at the joints on bamboo need to be whittled somewhat smooth for the sake of accuracy, and this is time consuming.

Regardless of what material you use for the arrow shaft, fletching (feathers, vanes) must be applied for the sake of accuracy. The fletching must be applied in such a way to impart a slight spin on the arrow in flight.

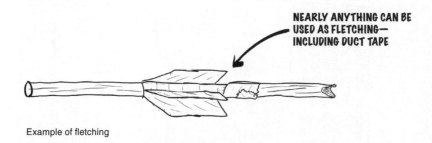

NEARLY ANYTHING CAN BE USED AS FLETCHING— INCLUDING DUCT TAPE

Example of fletching

Almost anything could be used as fletching—electrical tape, paper, actual feathers, and so forth, are all possibilities. Here, duct tape was fashioned as fletching. Without fletching of some sort, the arrow may veer off in almost any direction. Notching is accomplished by cutting the bamboo in two opposing cuts.

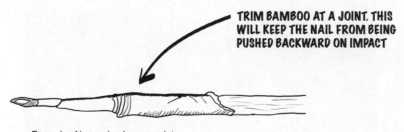

TRIM BAMBOO AT A JOINT. THIS WILL KEEP THE NAIL FROM BEING PUSHED BACKWARD ON IMPACT

Example of improvised arrow point

The point is a nail. There is a bamboo joint just behind the nail (under the duct tape) that keeps the nail from being pushed backward on impact. Accuracy can be improved by carefully skimming off the bumpy joints along the shaft.

Impact of homemade arrow in plywood.

Impact of homemade arrow through a water bottle. Most useful with small game (rabbits) at close range.

HUNTING SPEARS—As with the discussion of slingshots earlier, everyone on the planet knows what a spear is and how it is used.

Homemade hunting spear with tip fashioned from scrap metal.

Their usefulness would be extremely limited in most parts of North America. Most of us would not be accurate enough to hit small game such as rabbits with a spear.

There are a few areas in some southern states where wild hogs have simply overrun the land and have populated the woods with literal herds of their species. In an area like this, a spear might be of some limited use.

Impact of homemade spear in plywood.

Though I have not personally done it, I have known hunters who sit in tree stands, waiting for a hog, deer, or whatever, to walk beneath him and then take the animal down with his spear. Again, this would only be worthwhile in an area that was literally loaded with game.

In an actual survival situation, sharpening your spear as much as possible, not to mention slimming down and smoothing your spear shaft, would aid in deeper penetration into the game.

SECTION TWO
PLANNING AHEAD FOR WORST-CASE SCENARIOS

CHAPTER FOUR
BUG-OUT BAGS AND SURVIVAL PACKS

I know I'm beginning to sound like a broken record, but almost everything is this book is situation oriented. Bug-out bags and survival packs are no different.

For example, in my personal survival pack—a fairly large backpack—I don't have any snare wire. Why not? Because in the area where I live and usually travel, small game is not overly abundant. But streams, lakes, and ponds are almost everywhere. Therefore, my own personal survival pack has more water resource (fishing) items than anything else.

If, on the other hand, I lived in desert areas of western Texas instead of east Texas, my backpack would have some entirely different items in it. The basics (fire starting, shelter, and so forth) might be the same, but hydration items would be more important than fishing gear.

Anyone traveling in an area like Yellowstone in the dead of winter would certainly have different items in their pack. Cold weather items would be a plus in that situation, whereas in the same area in the hot summer, those items would just be something useless to carry around.

The gist of all this is that none of the following survival packs is "carved in stone" or "gospel."

Everything from your traveling area and its remoteness, the time of year, your ability to get help, and on and on, are all factors in what you might want in your pack. Adapt to your situation.

In most literature of this kind, a bug-out bag and a survival pack are two different things. I use the terms synonymously because I use the same pack for both purposes. Traditionally, a bug-out bag, in addition to equipment and gear, also has food and water. I have a separate pack with food and water.

My backpack is geared for eastern Texas, where we have moderate winters. I leave items in my pack that will last all year round (no food or water), and it's ready at a moment's notice, since nothing in it is perishable. We are all more likely to take a bug-out bag with us if it is already packed, rather than having to gather the items up at the spur of the moment.

My pack also has "comfort" items for a day trip to the river or lake and "useful" items if that day trip unexpectedly turns into a "stranded overnight" situation. I also keep some survival items that I hope never to use.

Your pack should be easily carried in one hand and shouldn't weigh more than twenty pounds.

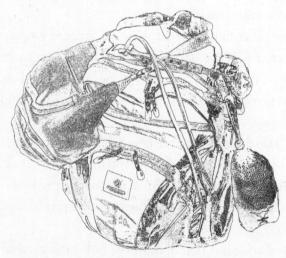

Bug-out bag ready to go

These are the items in the pack. Most have obvious uses, and don't require much explanation.

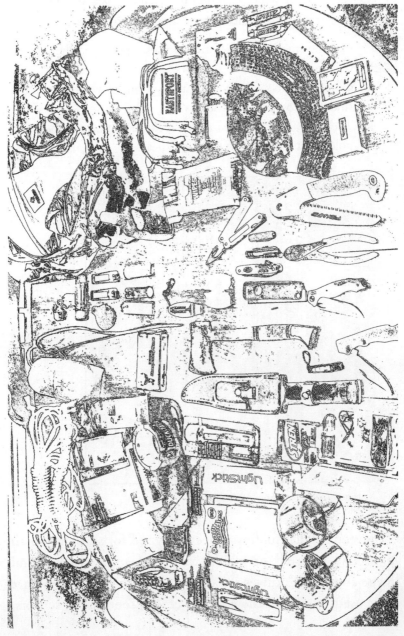

Entire contents of pack

EDGE TOOLS—Too many edge tools are better than none or only one. Since there really is no "all-purpose" cutting utensil, I keep several in my pack.

A large, heavy-bladed survival knife, a hand axe, and a folding saw are all good for the following generally obvious uses:

1. Cutting small saplings for constructing a tarp shelter
2. Cutting fishing poles
3. Chipping (or sawing) off small splints of wood for either tinder or cooking fire chunks
4. The large, heavy-bladed survival knife can be attached to a pole and used as an improvised spear.

Numerous knives, hand axe, folding saw

Several smaller folding knives are good for skinning small game, like squirrels or rabbits, or for cleaning fish. Several "Swiss army-type" knives are always a plus, since they can have other useful items on them like tweezers, toothpicks, scissors, and the like. I keep at least one utility tool. These are great if only for the pliers. There is always something you need pliers for.

If you only want to put one knife in your pack, I would go with the heavier hunting knife. It's a little awkward for skinning small game but is still usable for that, and it's also good for heavier work (chopping and so on), whereas a small folding knife is not.

A close second choice would be the utility tool, since most normally have a knife blade on them, along with numerous other attachments, especially the pliers.

If you do decide to just have a one-knife kit, make sure it is quality steel like a Saburo survival knife. My survival knife keeps an edge so sharp I am almost afraid to use it. A cheap, half-sharp, survival knife is not a lot better than a shop rock. Again, however, having several edge tools is better than just one, no matter how good the one is.

FIRE-STARTING MATERIALS—Like knives, having more than one of these items doesn't hurt. I keep containers of matches, a flint/magnesium bar kit, and several Bic-type lighters. Having

several fire-starting items instead of just a few matches gives you back up in case the matches get wet or something on that order. The reserve items might keep you from having to struggle to build a bow and spindle set in the woods.

Fire-starting materials

SHELTER ITEMS—A fair-sized (10-foot square) plastic tarp with grommets around the edges will make a pretty good "have-to" shelter, if needed. Some hooded plastic ponchos (even garbage bags) and emergency blankets are also good to have.

You will almost certainly need some cordage for setting up the tarp. Heavier rope might come in handy. I also suggest carrying around duct tape for repair jobs.

Shelter items

LIGHTING ITEMS—Candles are handy for

1. Getting set up in the dark if you have no other light source,
2. Lighting stubborn tinder going for a fire by giving you a steady flame once lit. At times, you can get a fire going with a candle that you can't with a match, because the match won't burn long enough.
3. Using as a heat source. Candles give off a surprising amount of heat for cold weather use.
4. Heating a small can of stew, in a pinch.

Other light sources may include light sticks (they don't put out light like a Q-beam flashlight by any means, but they are handy for quick lighting) or a flashlight with fresh batteries (for obvious reasons).

Lighting items

UTENSILS AND CONTAINERS—I only carry a couple of metal cups. If I am actually planning on being in the woods for long enough that cooking is an issue, I will bring the food and cooking utensils together in a separate pack.

The two cups I normally carry in my bug-out bag are really for unexpected emergencies. Their two main uses would be first, to boil small amounts of water for drinking; and second, to cook small bits of food (rabbit stew).

Mess kit

FISHING EQUIPMENT—In a basic pack like this, not much fishing equipment is necessary. You can cut your own pole if convenient, hand fish with no pole, or use the throw line option.

I have the following in my emergency fishing kit:

- 20 small lead split weights
- Spool of monofilament fishing line
- 15 assorted size hooks
- Fish stringer
- Snake bite kit

Fishing Items

MISCELLANEOUS ITEMS—This is stuff I can get by without but that I keep in my pack to make an unexpected stay in the woods a little more comfortable.

Toothbrushes, toothpaste, plastic toothpicks, a bar of soap, insect repellent, poison ivy cream, toilet wipes, wad of paper towels, and a deck of cards are just a few of hundreds of comfort items that might be important to you.

Miscellaneous comfort items

One of those survival whistles that are usually plastic and have a compass, magnifying glass, and thermometer on them could come in handy. If you get lost, the whistle would be heard from great distances, regardless of the other items.

Whistle combination tool

First-Aid Items—It wouldn't hurt to at least have a basic store-bought first aid kit in your pack.

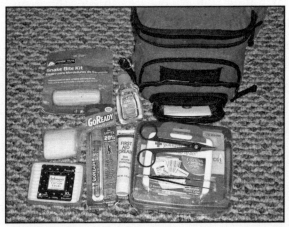

Basic first-aid kit

My kit contains the following:
- Snake bit kit with scalpel
- Strip of gauze
- Scissors
- Numerous sizes and kinds of bandages

- Anti-bacterial hand wash
- Disinfectant wipes
- First aid cream
- Tweezers
- Q-tips
- Bar of soap
- Insect repellent.

This kit is relatively limited. A larger kit would always be better, if feasible.

Outdoor and survival packs can range in size to be tiny enough to fit in a skoal snuff can that can be put in your hip pocket, to fanny-pack size, to small-pack size, to backpack size (as we have been discussing), to large mountain-pack size. They can be made especially to keep in your car, with fishing tackle and hunting gear, in case of transportation emergencies, or even attached to your hiking staff if you are a hiker. The items and variation involved is endless.

Just remember the Golden Rule of bug-out bags: If you don't have it with you, it's not a lot of help. If being small and compact (fanny-pack size) means you're more likely you will take your survival pack with you (as opposed to leaving it at home), then that might be the way to go. Adapt it for your use.

CHAPTER FIVE
Thinking Ahead and Stockpiling Supplies

Regardless of what you might hear from some sources, having a reserve of supplies is a good idea. I've read articles recently from a number of sources that were very negative on stockpiling food, medicines, and general supplies. They all claim that nothing bad will happen and that supplies will always be available. Some even lay a "guilt trip" on us about how stockpiling supplies will cause shortages and so forth.

I hope they are right about nothing bad happening, and I hope supplies are always available. I further hope these supplies are always available at some reasonable price and that I have reasonable monetary resources with which to buy them.

But our forefathers have long had a history of having stores of food and supplies in reserve. It is just common sense.

And, regardless of what the bloggers and pundits say, things do happen. Local weather disasters like tornadoes and hurricanes wreak havoc on supply lines for short periods of time. A flu pandemic (or something worse) could devastate supply deliveries for who knows how long. Another terrorist attack like 2001 could have unknown but far reaching and terrible effects. Everyone's most prevalent fear—a national socioeconomic collapse like the one in 1929—is possible. I hope it doesn't happen, but systems do sometimes break down.

What items a person should stockpile and how much is left open to the individual's own circumstance.

At a bare minimum, everyone needs a couple of weeks' supply of food, medicine, and water to get you through most weather-related power outages and most short-term emergencies.

On the other end of the scale, some prefer to have huge, room-size pantries with a year's worth of food, water, and medicines.

Most of us will be somewhere in between because first, we simply don't have the storage capacity in our homes; and second, we don't have the available cash to stockpile that much.

Regardless of details, there are a few basic items that everyone would feel more comfortable having available in their homes in the event of an emergency, whether it be short lived or long term.

Obviously, these are general categories, not a detailed list.

- Food
- Medicines and vitamins
- Water
- Emergency gear
- Money

If the emergency turns into a more long-term dilemma, other items might come in handy. Again, at this point, these are general categories, not a list. Detailed lists will follow.

- Gasoline
- Guns and ammunition
- Water filtration ability
- Medicines/first aid
- Food
- Tools
- Seeds

Although stockpiling consists of many different kinds of supplies, most of us first think of food.

If possible, keeping several storage areas filled with non-perishable food supplies would make anyone feel a lot more comfortable should an emergency arise. A typical closet pantry contains water, canned vegetables, fruits, soups, and meats, as well as preserves, salmon, spices, crackers, and bottled juices.

In setting up food storage in your home, there are a few do's and don'ts that are generally obvious but still deserve mentioning.

Do

1. Buy the same size containers of food that you normally use on a daily or weekly basis. If your family is small, buying the huge cans of vegetables that cafeterias keep in stock is probably a bad idea. The odds are that much more of that container will go to waste, especially if you are eating it during a power outage where the leftovers can't be refrigerated.

2. Buy items that you eat on a regular basis. You will periodically need to eat out of your stockpile and resupply in order to keep your stockpile fresh. This is less likely to happen if you buy foods you don't really like just to have something in an emergency.

3. Store inside your home and not in an non-air-conditioned garage or similar place. Most canned and dried foods last much longer when they are kept out of hot areas like these. And once canned food freezes and thaws, it is worthless. Something to keep in mind if you live where there are cold winters.

4. Reach in the back of the shelves and buy the product with the expiration date as far in the future as possible when shopping for your stockpile supplies.

5. Store your food by expiration date. For example, you might have several boxes (or shelves) labeled with the expiration dates. 2009, 2010, 2011, and so on. Try to empty the 2009 box first. That doesn't mean you can't grab something out of the box that doesn't expire until 2011 if you need to. The

point is, you don't really care when you bought the item—you want to know how long it will be good for.

6. Include items for members of your family that may have special needs. For example, infant foods, or food/medicines for diabetics.

7. Include vitamins, even if you don't normally take them. In a situation where you might not be receiving enough nutrition, general purpose vitamins might help.

DON'T

1. Store bulky paper goods like paper towels in your stockpile. You can't eat them, they take up a lot of room, and in dire economic straits, they would probably be the first thing you quit buying anyway. An exception to this might be if you had one of those room-sized pantries discussed earlier.

2. Go completely overboard and store so much you could never eat it all. There could be exceptions to this. Food could be a bartering item in a long term survival situation.

3. Store your food by the date you bought it. For example, let's say you bought two cans of beef stew on the same day. When you get home, you noticed one expires in 2010, and the other was much fresher, with an expiration date of 2013. Obviously, the date you bought the item is really irrelevant. Store items by the expiration date.

4. Wait for a sale to stock up. Build up your stockpile a little at a time if necessary, but make a start.

Organize storage by expiration date and category. Store your food in cardboard boxes that are not so large as to be too heavy. Keep an easy-to-read list of the boxes' inventory right on the box. When adding to or taking from the box, adjust the list on the box with a magic marker.

A word about freshness and expiration dates before we get to our food lists. Food labeling in the United States is mostly voluntary. There are a few items for infants that federal law demands be labeled with expiration dates. A few states have laws saying dairy

Box of food storage with labeled inventory

products must be pulled from the shelves on their expiration date. That's about it. The rest is voluntary.

EXPIRATION DATE: Pretty much says what it means. Anytime after this date, you're eating at your own risk.

SELL BY DATE: The date that the product is at the end of its peak freshness. It will still be edible for some time thereafter, but quality or taste will begin to suffer.

BEST BY DATE: Not a safety issue. This date recommends the last date to use for peak freshness.

GUARANTEED FRESH DATE: Not a safety issue. Fresh through this date, but gradually more stale as time goes by.

USE BY DATE: Pretty much the same as expiration date. May be okay for some time after, but this date is what the manufacturer has recommended.

SHELF LIFE OF BASIC ITEMS

Several things surprised me about thirty years ago when I first began experimenting with stockpiling food for an emergency.

I once thought the shelf life of some items, like dried pinto beans, were virtually unlimited. They're not. Generally, the expiration date of such items is only about one year—two at most.

The shelf life of bottled water is equally short—typically less than a year. Recent studies have shown that bacteria may build up in water even sooner than that on the store shelf, depending on conditions. This is why I recommend having water on hand and, equally important, having containers on hand to fill should you be able to do so.

The shelf life of food products might not be what you would ordinarily guess. This list has been compiled from practical experience checking the expiration dates on various items in grocery stores.

MEDICINE AND FIRST AID	
Vitamins	6 mo. to 1 year
OTC pain medicines	1 year
OTC stomach medicines	1 year
Alcohol/first aid items	Unlimited
WATER AND BEVERAGES	
Bottled Water	6 mo. at most
Bottled and canned juices	1 to 1½ years
Canned vegetable juices	1 to 1½ years
Canned milk	1 to 2 years
FRESH FOOD ITEMS	
Fresh fruits and vegetables	A few days only
Bread	A few days only
CANNED FOOD:	
Canned meats	Up to 4 years
Canned soups	2 years
Canned vegetables	3 years
Canned fruits	2 years
BREAKFAST ITEMS	
Dry cereal/cereal bars	4 mo.

Oatmeal	8 mo.
Syrups	Unlimited
Peanut butter	1 to 2 years
BAKING SUPPLIES	
Salt/Sugar	Unlimited
Flour	2 years
Corn Meal	2 years
Powdered Milk	Less than 1 year
DRIED FOOD	
Dried beans	Less than 2 years
Dried fruits	1 to 2 years
SNACKS AND NUTS	
Crackers/cookies	2 months
Trail mixes	1 year
Canned nuts	1 to 2 years
Chips	A few weeks

FOOD LIST

As with the survival packs earlier, this food list is not carved in stone or offered as gospel. Vary it to your own situation.

This list is made keeping in mind items with long shelf lives and have no need of freezing, refrigeration, or elaborate preparation.

Canned Foods—Vegetables
Corn
Hominy
Green beans
Carrots
Mixed vegetables
Spinach
Numerous types of peas
Numerous types of beans
New potatoes
Tomatoes

Canned Food—Meat
Chili
Ham
Spam
Chicken
Tuna
Chow mein
Beef stew
Ravioli
Spaghetti and meatballs
Corned beef

Chicken and dumplings	Jerky
Meat Soups	Dried cereals
	Oatmeal
Canned Food—Fruit	Cereal bars
Numerous varieties	Trail mix items
	Spaghetti and macaroni
Crackers	Non-food cooking items
Peanut butter	Cooking oil, flour, corn
Dried fruit	meal, salt, pepper, sugar,
Dried pinto beans	and assorted spices.
Popcorn	Coffee and tea bags

WATER

Stock at least a gallon a day per person and as much as storage allows over that. Again, it is likely that any societal problem that might occur will give us enough warning to collect water, so have empty containers ready to fill.

Also, any breakdown in municipal services, if it goes on long enough, might entail your needing some water filtration ability. Rather than having to build a make-shift filter from spare parts, having a commercially made filter ready would be a big plus. Even a simple gravity fed Brita-type filter (with extra pads) would be a good idea for your stockpile.

EMERGENCY GEAR

Stockpiling gear prevents you from having to gather it from multiple sources when the need arises and prevents you from having to do without it because you can't buy it. For example, generators after a storm or hurricane are almost always sold out quickly.

As with the survival packs discussed earlier in this book, emergency gear is more likely to be used (or taken with you) if it is already gathered up and in place when the need arises.

Emergency gear, like everything, is situation oriented. However I would classify gear in two general categories: around-the house-gear and outdoor gear for retreating to more primitive areas, even temporarily.

Around-the-house gear would be items that could be used while still living in your home. Generally, these would be items that would help you during power outages and similar inconveniences. For example:

- Matches
- Flashlights (and extra batteries)
- Candles
- Kerosene lamps (and fuel)
- Portable camp stove (and fuel)
- Radio (with batteries or, even better, one of those hand cranked rechargeable radios)
- Firewood (even if you don't have a fireplace)
- Ice chest
- Cell phone
- Water filter (Brita or similar)

On the "nice to have" list, although not all that critical, might be items like

- Battery-operated TVs
- Portable generators (with fuel)
- Games that don't require electricity (chess, Monopoly, cards, and so forth).

Outdoor gear to stockpile would be items you keep ready to be picked up at a moment's notice. These would mostly be commercially made items that you could use to make reaping outdoor resources much easier than the primitive items discussed earlier in this book. They would be items that could be used for brief trips to the wild in order to claim some resources, or survival in a full scale retreat to the wilderness to avoid local social upheavals. They might be items like:

- Traditional Fishing Gear—Hooks, lines, rod/reel, poles, weights, lures, stringers, baits, and so forth.

These would be the "normal" fishing items one might buy at an outdoor store for a traditional fishing trip.

- **FISHING TRAPS AND NETS**—Both ready-made traps, and trap materials as discussed earlier in this book. Also, nets (even minnow seines) could be invaluable. Netting and trapping are simply efficient when compared to traditional fishing. On a ratio of energy expended versus resources gained, trapping and netting are difficult to beat compared to traditional sport fishing. Pay special attention to the cloverleaf trap for a marvel of efficiency.

- **CAMPING GEAR**—Traditional items such as tents, sleeping bags, lanterns and fuel, and the like, all in one large duffel bag. The tent is probably the most important for most of us. Be sure to include at least one backpack-sized container full of pots, pans, skillets, salt, pepper, camp coffee pot, can openers, cups and plates (plastic or metal preferably—nothing breakable), and utensils. A dish pan with detergent comes in handy too. (Note: this gear does not contain food items and can be left packed in storage almost indefinitely.) Food items and your survival pack items will be brought separately.

GUNS AND AMMUNITION FOR HUNTING AND DEFENSE

A discussion of the merits of guns and ammo could take up several entire books. Everyone has favorites and reasons why they are right and you are wrong.

Let it suffice to say that you need to adapt whatever gun (or guns) you have available to whatever game will be available in the area you most likely will be.

Like knives, there really is no "perfect" or "all purpose" gun. That is why most avid outdoorsmen have several different kinds.

Perhaps the best advice on guns is to use what you have. Let me give an example of an acquaintance that had me recently analyze his gear (including a few guns he had) and make suggestions.

The gentleman I was helping was about sixty years old and had about ten different guns that he had accumulated over a lifetime. He was not a gun enthusiast, particularly. Most of the guns that he owned he did not buy himself. He had inherited several of them from his parents and grandparents and had had a couple of them since he was young.

I picked out five and told him that in my opinion, I wouldn't go out and buy anything. I would use what he had for a number of reasons.

He happened to have a Remington Nylon 66 semi-automatic .22 rifle. I think I read somewhere that these aren't even made anymore, but they are one of the best and most trouble free .22 rifles ever made. I owned one myself many years ago. For hunting small game like squirrels or rabbits, they are superb. For home defense, they will spit out lead so fast, they almost sound like a machine gun, and they do so without jamming. Last, .22 ammunition is both cheap and extremely common.

He had an inexpensive pump 12-gauge shotgun. It isn't valuable, but it's very useful for both a variety of hunting situations and home defense. For hunting, you can use it for anything from quail to deer, depending of what size shot you use. It is very versatile. For home defense, not many people will keep coming into your home if they are staring into the barrel of a shotgun. And, much like the .22, the ammunition is commonly available.

He also owned a .225 varmint rifle. It shoots a small but high speed bullet and is capable of hitting basket ball–sized targets from hundreds of yards away. In essence, it is a poor man's sniper rifle. It would be good for shooting in open country where it is difficult to get close to wild game. The ammunition isn't common, but the owner had stocked up and had an abundance of it.

The owner had a couple of pistols, as well. And although

neither of them would have been my choice if I were buying a pistol, I recommended that he use what he had rather than going out and spending a lot of money.

A .38 is fine for personal and home defense and small enough

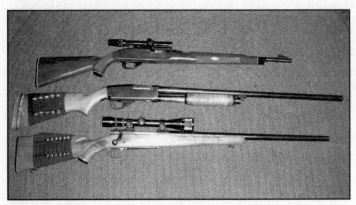

Shotgun and rifles

to be carried concealed on your person. A .22 pistol would be marginal for the same purposes but would allow for more practice, as the ammunition is much cheaper.

All in all, in this gentlemen's case, what he already had was good enough. Not perfect, but usable.

On the other hand, if you have no gun whatsoever to your

Pistols

name and you wish to buy a good, general-purpose gun, the most "all-purpose" gun I have ever owned was an over/under rifle shotgun combination.

I once owned a Savage 24-c over/under rifle shotgun combination and wish I still had it today. (Are you listening, Savage Arms? I'm not proud; you could send me one!)

It had a 30/30 rifle on the top barrel and a 12-gauge shotgun on the bottom barrel.

What I like about these guns:

1. Their adaptability to conditions in the field. You can either fire the shotgun barrel or the rifle barrel at a split seconds notice.
2. You can vary the shotgun ammunition by carrying different types in your hunting vest. For example, you can carry #8 shot in the barrel for squirrels and birds and the like, but have a few OO buckshot shells in your vest in case you stumble across a deer or wild pig (bigger game). The buckshot might allow you to shoot at a moving deer that you might be reluctant to try with the rifle.
3. The 30/30 will take care of most North American game. It does not have the punch of a 30.06, of course, but nonetheless, is plenty good for whitetail deer, wild pigs, and so on.
4. In a pinch, the 30/30 will knock down a squirrel or rabbit if it is out of shotgun range. It's a little on the overkill side, but usable.

MONEY

When most of us think of the work "stockpile," we think of boxes or bags of supplies. Certainly, most of us have too little monetary resources to "stockpile."

Nonetheless, having some cash put away around the house is a good idea. Preferably not a lot. And more preferably, no one else needs to know about it.

Having a little cash (in small bills) will make you feel more comfortable if the electricity is out in your area and none of the stores can take credit cards.

There could be situations develop where merchants won't take checks or credit cards, but cash would still be welcome.

Be cautious. Like everything, there is a down side. Money around the house can be misplaced, stolen, lost in a fire, or some such disaster.

Longer Term Dilemma Stockpile Items

If the social fabric of the nation really went downhill, and the economy just "tanked" as it did in 1929, more long term items would be good to have. Since no one really knows the future, having items to barter with for things you need can't hurt.

Earlier in our nation's history, bartering was significantly more prevalent than it is now. We've all heard the stories about how the farmers on the frontier paid the doctor with chickens and eggs. Goods for services. Goods for other goods.

Common bartering items that are most likely to be in short supply during such a time of social unrest might include:

- GUNS—There is always a demand, even in good times. There would be more demand in bad times.

- AMMUNITION—There is always a demand, exactly as in guns above.

- GASOLINE—Hard for most of us to store unless we happen to live in the country and have one of those 200-gallon gravity fed tanks. Safety issues relate to storing gas in your garages where a spark might ignite the fumes. Be cautious.

- WATER FILTRATION ABILITY OR EQUIPMENT—In a long-term event, water filtration and purification will be a necessity. Having either the equipment or the skills could be a plus.

- MEDICINES (OTC) AND FIRST-AID SUPPLIES—in

a long term event, standard over-the-counter medicines could become hard to find. Thermometers, blood pressure gauges, Tylenol, Advil, and other basic items of this nature could be used to barter.

- Food—Obviously, common sense comes into play here.

- Tools—Other useful items always in high demand, even in good times. In bad times, hand tools could possibly become more valuable than they might otherwise.

- Seeds for planting—Things would really have to go downhill in our civilization for several months in order for seeds to become a barter item, but it could happen. I hope it doesn't, though.

- Skills—Although not exactly something you could stockpile, skills of all sorts could become valuable. Especially knowledge of growing crops, gathering resources, purifying water, and so on.

SECTION THREE
THE REALLY WORST-CASE SCENARIO

CHAPTER SIX

RETREATING TO WILDERNESS AREAS FOR SAFETY

As I have repeated many times, I hope nothing bad will happen and that we can all live out our lives in relative comfort. But so many different things could happen, and a list of possible threats will be discussed later in this chapter.

Our reaction to each of these many possible threats will vary depending on our circumstances. The number of possible scenarios (threat versus our reaction) is absolutely endless. But regardless of what the threat is, our survival could come down to a relatively simple question:

"Do I stay at home and weather the event, or do I retreat to a wilderness area until it is over?:

In actual decision making and implementation at the time, there is no simple answer; it is a complex issue. In being prepared, however, it is a simple issue. Do both.

HISTORY OF SURVIVAL CULTURE

In the late 1950s, the survivalist culture centered on two things: nuclear attack and the threat of the Soviet Union.

Fallout shelters were the most talked about item of the day. They were advertised on television for sale commercially. News reports demonstrated how these shelters were built and installed in "average people's" back yards, like a swing set for the kids. Fallout shelters were advertised as the "latest thing" in convenience by the sellers. Note that none of the sellers talked about how miserable living in one of these holes in the ground would actually be.

During the 1960s, the basic threat was still considered the same, but retreating to sparsely populated remote areas were considered as a more viable option.

During this time, maps started circulating about possible nuclear target sites in our country. Then maps of coverage areas of fallout from such strikes appeared, even taking prevailing winds into the equation. Even maps of areas that would likely not be affected as severely turned up. Fallout shelters didn't disappear from the survival culture, but they now had a more backseat role.

It was during this time that terms like "retreat technology" entered the American vernacular. There were two general options: battening down (staying put), or bugging out (leaving). Other terms included BOV (bug-out vehicle), BOL (bug-out location), and BOB (bug-out bag; sometimes called a 72-hour survival kit).

By the 1970s, in addition to the threats already mentioned, two more threats were added to the mix: Germ warfare (biological plagues) and a complete economic and social collapse of society (from myriad possible causes).

On September, 11, 2001, we discovered a new threat. Few had considered, prior to that dreadful day, an enemy would use commercial airliners as missiles to attack our nation. And shortly thereafter, few of us had thought of using crop dusters being used to spread poisons over our cities.

By 2008, the worry was (and still is, as of this writing) that we could experience a complete economic collapse and thus a societal collapse. Yet our government insists on running up a few trillion more in debt to solve the problem.

So what are the present threats out there? It would be a long list. I have chosen to leave out of the lists such things as asteroid impacts and alien invasions. We have a lot of more likely threats. I have also chosen to leave out biological warfare threats, as dealing with these could be a complete book in its own right. All most of us could do short term would be to poly and duct tape a room in our house, like we did during the anthrax scare.

POTENTIAL THREATS

The following lists is both short and longer term threats, in no particular order:

NATURAL DISASTERS
- Floods
- Hurricanes/tornadoes
- Earthquakes
- Blizzards
- Famine
- Drought

MAN/SOCIETY-INDUCED THREATS
- Terrorist attack
- Nuclear detonation
- Electromagnetic Pulse Attack
- Simple power outages
- Release of toxic chemicals
- Financial system collapse
- Governmental system collapse

THREAT RESPONSE

So, what do you do? Hang tough or head for the hills? As far as preparation goes, prepare to do both. Most of us will hang in there at home as long as possible, but having an "out" if needed is always a plus.

The scale of the threat along with its expected duration dictates the decision process of whether to stay or retreat.

Consider the following:

STAY-AT-HOME ADVANTAGES:

- Shelter that you are familiar with and comfortable using
- Access to bedding and comforts of home
- Familiar with area nearby as to securing supplies
- More familiar with people nearby
- Your stockpile won't have to be transported elsewhere
- Home is a lot less boring than most emergency shelters
- You can evacuate later if necessary
- You can probably defend yourself better if it comes to that
- Most people live near at least some relatives; possible aid
- Even if you lose power, most of your freezer food can be utilized and will not go to waste.

STAY-AT-HOME DISADVANTAGES:

1. The threat may turn out to be much worse than anticipated
2. Evacuating later may be impossible
3. If everyone else is gone, you may feel isolated and fearful
4. If utility services are out, home is not the same

Again, the severity of the threat coupled with how long it is expected to last will dictate your decision.

However, given that at some point retreating may be something you have to do, what do you look for in a retreat location?

There are two general schools of thought about retreating: (1) the buddy system, and (2) the remote wilderness retreat.

BUDDY SYSTEM

In the buddy system, you and a relative, associate, or friend agree in advance to be each other's retreat. This system is excellent for localized disasters such as hurricanes. It would be less valuable for nationwide calamities because likely both of you would be affected by the same disaster.

In using the buddy system, consider the following parameters:

1. You and the buddy need to be 100 to 150 miles apart to lessen the chance that the threat affects you both.
2. You and your buddy must be reachable on one tank of gas is possible, as gas (and hotels) are often unavailable after a disaster.
3. If one of you lives in a big city, the other needs to be in rural area.
4. If one of you is in a coastal area, the other needs to be inland.

The disadvantage of the buddy system is that since each of you is using the others home as an retreat, if the calamity is widespread, it could likely affect both of you.

But it does have a few advantages:

1. In the event of a localized disaster, you have a solid destination; you aren't just aimlessly running away. This makes you less fearful.
2. You don't have to maintain a separate house in another area for emergencies.
3. Your buddy will provide much of the supplies you will need, and vice versa, of course.

REMOTE WILDERNESS RETREATS

By far, the remote wilderness retreat is generally more usable, regardless of what the threat is. This is not as true for the buddy system because you are both using your homes as each other's retreat.

The term "remote wilderness" is accurate, yet misleading. A retreat needs to be "remote" only in the sense that it is not visible from the nearest road and as few people as possible would really think of going there. It can be only a few yards off some back country road within a few miles of the nearest town as long as it is relatively isolated, and it's a place no one else is likely to go. It doesn't have to be 60 miles back up in the hills.

And "wilderness" is also a relative term. Your retreat doesn't have to be particularly deep forest. It just needs to be "out of sight, out of (other people's) mind."

RETREAT CHARACTERISTICS—Look for a site with the following characteristics:

1. In the country but less than 5 miles from the nearest small town and at least one tank of gas away from the nearest large city.
2. Acreage without a house. This would seem a disadvantage, but it isn't. In retreat areas, rarely visited houses are almost always broken into, vandalized, or worse. Sometimes squatters set up housekeeping and start living there. Drug producers sometimes set up meth labs or plant marijuana fields in remote areas that they don't own and thus can't be held accountable for. A camp trailer, or even tents, that you can take when you go, is a better answer. If there is a house there, someone is going to find it and do something to it.
3. Not visible from the nearest road. (In the photos on the following pages, both small lakes were built many years ago. Thus, even most locals, probably will not even be aware of the sites.
4. Not visible from the air. If you have small shedlike pavilion, make sure overhanging branches of trees cover it from above.
5. Available game. Squirrels, deer, wild pigs, and most important, fish.
6. Arable soil for growing a garden if the situation was long term.
7. Available water, especially in the summer.

See the following photos for examples of wilderness retreats.

This site has a small lake that receives water from a spring-fed creek. It features a small pavilion with a grill, table, and a few chairs. There is nothing else on-site year round for intruders to vandalize. It's a half mile from the nearest road and completely surrounded by forest. Few people are aware of its existence.

This same site also features nearby open land with moderately plentiful wildlife. There is enough area to grow vegetables if the situation became long term.

A different site: a beaver pond, also spring fed and not visible from the nearest road. The pine forest along the dam provides cool shade, even in 100-degree summers. The land nearby was farmed in the 1940s and could be again.

PRACTICAL ISSUES OF COST

Little in the way of expense is incurred if enough forethought is put into the matter of retreating.

It is not necessary to actually buy rural property with the features described.

Most of us have relatives or associates who have such rural property and never use it. Elderly relatives may have had some rural property in the family for many years and virtually never go there. They may have inherited it from Uncle Bob or Aunt Jo thirty years ago but have always lived in the city. Gaining permission to camp or visit such properties will generally be easy, especially from relatives.

In my own area, there are countless small parcels of rural land that are owned by people who live in the Dallas area and perhaps come down once a year to give the land a cursory glance. Generally, someone local who would occasionally visit and look after their property would be a welcome plus for these folks.

Of course, owning such a site would be even better. Having several such sites picked out in advance is a comforting feeling, whether you own them or not.

A small travel trailer, however, might be more difficult to borrow—even from relatives. A travel trailer, motor home, tent trailer, or some such "mobile" shelter might be something to consider buying if that is feasible for you.

If not, the most elaborate (and comfortable) camping type shelter that you can afford will make a long-term stay more bearable.

Like everything in this book, thinking through your possible reactions in advance and at least making some preparation will make life easier later.

CHAPTER SEVEN
PSYCHOLOGY OF SURVIVAL

I would like to relate three scenarios. The first two are true stories of events that did happen. The third is a story that almost surely will happen, to some degree. They all interrelate and delve into the psychology of surviving difficult times.

1. THE HUGH GLASS STORY

Hugh Glass's story is fairly well known. If you have seen the 1971 movie called *A Man in the Wilderness*, you have seen a fairly accurate version of the Hugh Glass story. The movie starred Richard Harris and John Huston, and it did (as movies always do) take some liberties, but it's moderately accurate.

His survival trek was famous while he was still alive; hence he literally became a living legend in his own time. Although Glass himself was not much of a talker, his survival story was so extraordinary it spread across the West. His story needed no embellishment. It was widely related to other frontiersmen at the time and even became part of tribal Native American folklore. A monument to Glass stands on the shores of the Shadehill Reservoir southwest of Shadehill, South Dakota, which says: "This altar to courage was erected by the Neihardt Club August 1, 1923, in memory of Hugh Glass who, wounded and deserted here, began his crawl to Ft. Kiowa in the fall of 1823."

Glass was with the William Ashley expedition in 1823 on a fur trading venture up the Missouri River. The expedition was composed of a group of about a hundred men, referred to later as Ashley's Hundred.

Some in the group were well known, or later became well known. These included John Fitzgerald, Jim Bridger, and Jedediah Smith.

In August, Glass was hunting alone for game to help feed the group in what would become South Dakota.

He surprised a mother grizzly bear with small cubs. The bear equally surprised him. The bear attacked Glass before he could even get his rifle up and shoot. He did manage to kill the bear with his hunting knife—no easy feat in itself—but found himself lying under the dead bear, badly mauled.

His companions found him by his screams. He was clawed, bitten, and badly mangled. His leg was broken, and much of his scalp was torn away. The flesh had been ripped away from part of his back, exposing some of his rib bones. There was virtually no where on his body where he wasn't clawed, ripped, or bitten. He was covered in blood.

When he soon lost consciousness, Ashley was certain Glass would not survive. It seemed impossible. He was simply too badly hurt. Even if he were in a big city hospital, he would still die.

Ashley asked for volunteers to stay with him until he died and bury him while the expedition moved on. They would catch up with the company later. It would likely just be hours—maybe minutes.

Seventeen-year-old Jim Bridger, who later became famous in his own right, volunteered. John Fitzgerald also agreed to stay behind with Glass.

The two immediately began digging Glass's grave, preparing for the inevitable.

The rest of the day passed, and Glass did not die. Nor did he die during the night.

Neither did he die on the second day.

Or the third.

When three days had passed, and Hugh Glass was still alive, Bridger and Fitzgerald grew uneasy. When a hostile band of Indians was seen nearby, Bridger and Fitzgerald panicked.

They covered Glass with a bear skin in the open grave, and piled a few sticks over him. They took his rifle and knife and left him for dead.

Still, Hugh Glass did not die. He woke up eventually with no gun, no knife, no supplies. His only protection from the wilderness was the bearskin.

He was alone, without food or water, completely unarmed, and 200 miles from the nearest help at Ft. Kiowa.

Later, Glass admitted to being driven by hate and revenge. He wanted to live to kill the two men who had deserted him.

Glass set his own broken leg and began crawling. It took him two months to crawl to the Cheyenne River. He ate roots and berries on the way and also managed to eat the raw meat from a wolf-killed bison.

At the Cheyenne River, he used a fallen tree as a raft and let the current carry him on to Ft. Kiowa. He had made a miraculous 200 mile journey of survival. It had taken months, but he had made it. Simply regaining his health took many more months.

It was nearly two years later when he caught up with Jim Bridger, intent on killing him. But he did not. Bridger was still only nineteen years old. Because of his youth, Glass forgave him.

Fitzgerald had, by this time, joined the army and was no longer in the area.

Glass lived another ten years after the 1823 incident.

2. THE ALASKAN PILOT

I read this story a while back and have tried to research it recently without any success. My memory of the event is hazy on the details, and I wanted to find news articles on the event, but could not. Regardless, the basic story is as follows:

A civilian pilot in Alaska had some sort of mechanical problem with his aircraft but managed to set it down on a frozen lake. He was completely uninjured.

He was, however, in the middle of nowhere, hundreds of miles from the nearest human. It was also about 20 below zero outside.

The sad and tragic part relates to what the pilot did not know. He did not know that an air traffic controller had seen him disappear from radar and had already dispatched help.

Perhaps the pilot was aware of the many cases where people slowly died while stranded in remote areas of vast Alaska. In many cases, they are simply never found, despite intense searches. Perhaps thoughts of a slow death had entered his mind. Perhaps not.

Regardless of his mind set, the pilot sat for a while and smoked a couple of cigarettes. He wrote a note, leaving it where it would be found, and committed suicide with a pistol he had with him in the cockpit.

The note said something like, "I cannot possibly survive in this cold. I am a dead man."

Rescuers, sent by the air controller, found his body and the note a short time later.

3. ECONOMIC/SOCIAL SURVIVAL PANIC

In 2008 and 2009, there were many articles about how the economic downturn in this country caused some people to exhibit extreme behaviors.

In one story, a highly paid but recently laid off employee shoplifted an expensive item simply because he felt he deserved it. He felt his situation wasn't his fault, and he was getting back at "them" for his deflated monetary situation. Had he still been employed, the thought of shoplifting probably would not have occurred to him.

Mental health experts predicted an increase in theft, drug use, general anxiety, depression, and even violence.

Regardless of how we respond to the possibility of living under different means than we've been accustomed, we need to, at the very least, be alert to potential extreme behaviors of others.

Living as most people had to do during the Great Depression would be a serious eye opener for us in today's world. Many younger people have grown up in a world where there has always been easy access to credit, and they have never really had to limit their purchases to what was absolutely necessary. It has always been possible to get that latest video game, new snazzy cell phone, big screen TV—the list could go on and on, but you get the idea.

When credit started diminishing and jobs disappearing, at least some people were expected to exhibit non-typical behavior.

Psychiatrist Timothy Fong at the UCLA Neuropsychiatric Institute and Hospital said: "I wouldn't be surprised if we see an up tick in crime, related to stealing. . . . I wouldn't be surprised if we see more workplace violence and more violence at the malls."

WHAT'S THE POINT?

It wouldn't seem like these three scenarios are related at all, but they illustrate the following point: being mentally prepared for whatever might happen will mitigate fear and panic.

In the Hugh Glass story, there can be little doubt that a mountain man like Glass was mentally prepared for surviving in the wilderness. It was ingrained in his nature by his life in wilderness areas.

Even badly injured and without equipment, Glass knew what had to be done. He, undoubtedly, knew how difficult and horrible the ordeal facing him was, but he was mentally prepared for the challenge.

If Glass had been a greenhorn with little or no knowledge of wilderness ways, he almost certainly would have given up and died. Why? Because he would have never dreamed of being in such a situation, and would have had no idea of any way to survive it. Fear and panic would have set in quickly. Lack of knowledge and forethought breeds panic, then despair.

In the Alaska pilot scenario, we will never know the real mind set of the pilot who tragically died by his own hand. However, his note did leave one thing extremely clear: he thought there was no way he could possibly survive.

Are we leaping to conclusions if we think he was simply not mentally prepared for his situation? Possibly. There is simply too much we don't know.

But one thing we do know is that had he simply sat tight and waited, the rescuers would have found him alive and well. If he had ever, prior to the crash, given much thought to what he would do in such a situation, he almost surely would have had a better plan than suicide.

And finally, being mentally prepared for the extreme behavior of others (in times of political unrest or economic downturn) will help mitigate any fear and panic that might otherwise befall you, not to mention that recognizing the symptoms of survival panic might help you personally from falling into the same depression.

Whether wilderness survival or social survival is the issue, thinking ahead of what might happen is always calming.

Thinking ahead and at least having a few ideas in mind will make anyone feel better if hard times do arrive, even if you don't actively start preparing and stockpiling.

And, obviously, if just having some ideas in mind of what you might do in the event of bad times makes you feel better, just think how much more self-confident you'll feel if you actively start your preparations.

ABOUT THE AUTHOR

Dale Martin grew up in rural East Texas in the 1950s and 60s spending countless hours and days in the woods enjoying the great outdoors. Learning outdoor skills was simply a natural by-product acquired over a life time.

In college, while earning a business degree, Dale took several courses in the anthropology of primitive cultures. He found the survival methods of primitive tribes both instructive and fascinating.

Dale's interest in primitive technology developed into several years of research into survival skills, animal snares, path guarding traps, improvised weapons, firearm silencer design, as well as other "off the beaten path" disciplines.

In 1987, Dale wrote *Trapper's Bible*, and followed that up with *Into the Primitive* in 1989. Both were how-to texts on primitive trapping, survival, and general outdoor lore. Now, some twenty plus years later, both books are still in print, and are still selling world wide. In 2009, *Trapper's Bible* was named by its publisher, Paladin Press, as one of its all-time best sellers. Both books have been positively reviewed many times by numerous magazines and outdoor writers, as well as featured on many survival book lists.

Dale has written numerous articles on military history, almost all of which were at the request of research sites on the internet.

He is the author of the privately published *The Shot*, the account of the most celebrated long range sniper shot of the American Civil War.

In the fall of 2001, Dale was contacted by *National Geographic* to write an article about deadfalls for their spin-off magazine *National Geographic Explorer*.

In 2007, Dale was contacted by the History Channel for his input into one of their *Modern Marvels* segments.

Aside from continuing his *Every Man's Guide to Outdoor Survival* series, Dale is working on several other book-length projects.

As of 2009, Dale lives with wife, Sue, in rural East Texas.

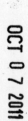